PEDAGOGICS OF LIBERATION

Before you start to read this book, take this moment to think about making a donation to punctum books, an independent non-profit press,

@ https://punctumbooks.com/support/

If you're reading the e-book, you can click on the image below to go directly to our donations site. Any amount, no matter the size, is appreciated and will help us to keep our ship of fools afloat. Contributions from dedicated readers will also help us to keep our commons open and to cultivate new work that can't find a welcoming port elsewhere. Our adventure is not possible without your support.

Vive la Open Access.

Fig. 1. Hieronymus Bosch, *Ship of Fools* (1490–1500)

PEDAGOGICS OF LIBERATION: A LATIN AMERICAN PHILOSOPHY OF EDUCATION. Copyright © 2019 by Enrique Dussel, David I. Backer, and Cecilia Diego. Introduction © 2019 by Linda Martín Alcoff. This work carries a Creative Commons BY-NC-SA 4.0 International license, which means that you are free to copy and redistribute the material in any medium or format, and you may also remix, transform and build upon the material, as long as you clearly attribute the work to the authors (but not in a way that suggests the authors or punctum books endorses you and your work), you do not use this work for commercial gain in any form whatsoever, and that for any remixing and transformation, you distribute your rebuild under the same license. http://creativecommons.org/licenses/by-nc-sa/4.0/

First published in 2019 by punctum books, Earth, Milky Way.
https://punctumbooks.com

ISBN-13: 978-1-950192-27-4 (print)
ISBN-13: 978-1-950192-28-1 (ePDF)

DOI: 10.21983/P3.0257.1.00

LCCN: 2019943219
Library of Congress Cataloging Data is available from the Library of Congress

Book design: Vincent W.J. van Gerven Oei

HIC SVNT MONSTRA

enrique dussel

PEDAGOGICS OF LIBERATION
PEDAGOGICS OF LIBERATION
PEDAGOGICS OF LIBERATION
PEDAGOGICS OF LIBERATION
PEDAGOGICS OF LIBERATION

a latin american philosophy of education
translated by david i. backer and cecilia diego
with a new preface and a foreword by linda martín alcoff

Contents

Foreword · 11
Translators' Preface · 31
Preface to the English Edition · 39

Preliminary Words · 47
§18   "The Other" as the Face of Pedagogics · 51
§48   Symbols and Pedagogics · 63
§49   Limits of a Dialectical Interpretation of Pedagogics · 81
§50   Meta-physical Description of Pedagogics · 105
§51   Economy and Pedagogics · 123
§52   Ethics of the Pedagogical Pro-ject · 141
§53   The Morality of Liberatory Pedagogical Praxis · 165

Bibliography · 191

Foreword

What if the schools in our communities are not, in fact, failing? What if the massive dropout rates, poor test scores, and poor skill sets that even graduating students sometimes leave school with are the actual systemic goal?

In a remarkable series of essays spanning the last forty-five years, the influential Argentinian-Mexican philosopher Enrique Dussel develops a pedagogics of liberation. We need first and foremost, he argues, a thorough and deep critique of those existing pedagogical practices and curriculum — Dussel calls them "educational praxes of domination" — that attempt to assimilate the poor of the global south or of first nations, by schooling them in the dominant westernized culture, its high art, its mainstream ideology, and its ethos of individualism and competition. The major result of such praxes is to impart a sense of failure among the poor, who of course constitute the majority of children and youth sitting in classrooms across the globe. And after inducing failure in these students, these "educational praxes of domination" then inculcate feelings of guilt and shame for having failed to successfully assimilate the dominant cultures of their exploiters.

Dussel's focus is on the pedagogy of Latin America, where, for example, even today less than half of low-income children complete nine years of school.[1] But his analysis of the effects of poverty and oppression and the persistent influence of colonialism will apply to the global South in general as well as to many communities, neighborhoods, and schools in the global North. Dussel's account applies everywhere that the children of laborers, of the racially oppressed, and of colonized cultures are forcibly subjected to the pedagogies of the dominant class, until they become so alienated that they leave school with, as he says, "a bitter taste of failure."[2]

In this introduction I will offer an analytical overview of Dussel's account that situates his contribution to the philosophy of education within his philosophy of liberation and within decolonial theory today. His writings on pedagogy have included both a critical and a reconstructive aspect, criticizing some of the canonical theory that is still practiced in colonial settings and settler contexts, and offering the contours of a reconstructed pedagogy that draws mainly from Latin American social theory but also engages with radical European philosophy, particularly the work of Emmanuel Levinas. But what Dussel primarily offers, I'll suggest, is a philosophical scaffolding or grounding for a decolonial pedagogy.

The decolonial turn is a relatively recent development in social theory so I begin with a brief account of the three major ways in which it is distinct from the older and more familiar postcolonial rubric that emerged in the 1970s. Dussel's work has been a major influence in the decolonial turn, and so this will also help introduce what is distinctive about his approach.[3]

---

1 See for example, the resources provided by the Inter-American Development Bank's "Graduate XXI" project: http://www.graduatexxi.org/en/recursos/. There is variation across countries yet a persistent lack of progress among poor children in rural areas.

2 All the quotations from Dussel's pedagogical essays come from this Backer/Diego translation.

3 See Nelson Maldonado-Torres, "Thinking Through the Decolonial Turn: Post-continental Interventions in Theory, Philosophy and Critique: An In-

Decolonial theory has emerged today in some measure as a reaction against what theorists saw as weaknesses in postcolonial thought. Postcolonial thought was and continues to be revolutionary in many of our disciplines in making the case for subaltern studies, in reaching beyond the nationalist narratives of colonial and even comprador elites, in putting the history of colonialism into the center of analysis in everything from literary theory to the European Enlightenment, and in mobilizing new thinking about the nature of domination and resistance that departs from or at least goes beyond Marxist categories.

Yet postcolonial thought had limitations, one of which was to continue to rely too much on European radical social theory, post-structuralist or postmodernist theory in particular. The critique often made, that postcolonial theorists were mostly working in institutions of the global North, is less important than the issue of where their theoretical resources are coming from. As Dussel has argued, the liberatory theories that enlivened the transformative hopes of much of the world throughout the nineteenth and twentieth centuries developed from basically five countries, all from the global North. These theories were borne of that local experience. Social conflict was not given a racial or ethnic cast, nor was the international division of labor a central analytic. Capitalism was not explained as a development out of, or alongside, colonialism, but as a replacement for European feudalism. As a result, liberatory social theories, including Marxism, developed no theory of race, no conceptualization of xenophobia, no critique of Eurocentrism, no concept of indigeneity, no analysis of the deep ties between culture and colonialism, and no analysis of the ways in which geographical hierarchies affect the making of theory itself.[4]

A few of the late-twentieth-century post-structuralist theorists began to attend (in a limited way) to race and colonialism but retain serious limitations in their understanding of colonial

---

troduction," *Transmodernity* 2, no. 1 (2011): 1–15.
4 See Linda Martín Alcoff, "Educating with a (De)Colonial Consciousness," *Lápiz* 1 (2014): 78–92.

categories of identity and histories of resistance. Their theories and concepts are grounded in European experiences, textual traditions, and local histories. Foucault's own analysis of the development of disciplinary techniques, for example, is seriously compromised by his focus on France as a nation emerging from inter-ethnic European conflicts rather than as a colonial empire. The European radical tradition is not only limited but its analyses have been flawed in ways decolonial scholars are now thinking through.

The debate that occurred over Edward Said's *Orientalism* when it was first published in 1978 is instructive. Critics (from the global North) charged Said with being too loose with Foucault, not being faithful, as it were, to Foucault's account. Said was bringing in issues about the subject position of orientalists, their national and racial identities. His analysis was quite nuanced but this still went against the grain of the early postmodern catechisms about the "death of the author." In other words, Said was not allowed to make his own use of Foucault, to take what he found helpful and leave behind the rest. He was enjoined to be a loyal subject. Certainly there are legitimate concerns about scholarship and theoretical eclecticism, yet Said was not writing a scholarly interpretation of Foucault's ideas but a critical analysis of orientalism.

Theoretical work on coloniality should make use of every available tool, but be aware of the hierarchies of citation that track the colonial world even in our current academic circulations. Quoting the latest European theorist continues to get more traction, and signifies more theoretical sophistication, than quoting theorists from the colonial world that may be relatively unknown in the academies of the north. Implicit bias works in the field of radical social theory.

A second major distinction between the decolonial and the postcolonial concerns is the time frame of analysis. Postcolonial scholarship began with the seventeenth century understandably as a project of subaltern studies in south Asia. Their focal point for colonialism was the British incursions which involved the creation of new colonial governments over territories that were not nationally unified, the importation of a class of administrators who would become overseers and bring their own European families with them rather than intermarrying with local people, and the particularity of British ideas about everything from common law to education and protestant values. The experience of colonization in the Americas that began two centuries earlier took quite a different form, involving sanctioned intermingling (from Cortés on), educational institutions as extensions of Catholic missions, relatively independent colonial governments with systems of land distribution and tributes organized as *gamonales* and *encomiendas,* and most importantly, a racialization of the labor force. From Columbus's journals we can chart the beginnings of a conversation about the labor potential of various groups that began to connect emerging ideas about human difference with behavioral dispositions and intellectual potential, not to mention social and even human status, all developed within a project of colonizing a labor force. Columbus did not encounter societies with racial concepts; the Europeans began to create the modern world racial system still in place today.[5] Hence, the constructions of racial difference preexisted the emergence of capitalism in the Americas, making it harder, if we start here, to dodge the fact that capitalism has been a racial capitalism since day one. Clearly, colonialism in the Americas had temporal priority in the grand scheme of European empires, putting into place techniques of bureaucratization, population management, governmentality, biopower, religious education, standardized time, and social reproduction that became the foundation for colonizing practices in Asia and Africa.[6] European colonialism was not monolithic. The Spanish and British styles sharply diverged over the question of intermarriage, for example. Yet the point remains that eighteenth-

---

[5] See Ramón Grosfoguel, "The Epistemic Decolonial Turn," *Cultural Studies* 21, nos. 2–3 (2007): 211–23.

[6] See Johannes Fabian, *Time and the Other: How Anthropology Makes Its Object* (New York: Columbia University Press, 2014).

century colonialisms built on and learned from the sixteenth century.

Most importantly, by beginning an analysis of the effects of coloniality with the conquest of the Americas rather than the incursions into South Asia, we have an altered understanding of the role of emerging ideas about race and the status of Europe as the vanguard of the human race. By the eighteenth century the Europeans understood themselves to have a distinct racial identity from those they colonized, and this understanding is apparent in both the liberal and the radical traditions from Locke, Kant, Hegel, Mill, and Marx. Contemporary radical European thought has yet to put either race or colonialism on its agenda.

The third difference between decolonial theory and postcolonial theory follows from these first two differences. Given the lacunae in radical European theory on many important topics, decolonial theorists today have a renewed interest in the theoretical developments that came along with the national liberation movements of the twentieth century. Postcolonial theory in some ways had to differentiate itself from the tradition of anti-colonial writing by Césaire, Fanon, Cabral, Senghor, Nkrumah, C.L.R. James, and others who had produced the main canon of theory up until the 1970s. Much of this tradition was itself engaged with radical European social theory and made good use of liberalism, existentialism, Marxism, and psychoanalysis. These particular nineteenth and mid-twentieth century European traditions of thought were ones that the later postcolonial theorists had a great deal of skepticism about, mainly for their subject- centered nature, inflated ideas about individual agency, and historical progressivism. So for some decades this rich canon of mid-century anti-colonial thought fell out of favor and was rarely taught or debated.

Decolonial theorists today are taking a new look at this canon. The point is not to revive and revere it intact. Its omission of gender and sexuality, weak intersectional analysis, and assumption of subject-centered nationalist projects merits ongoing criticism. And yet the texts themselves belie simplistic readings. So there is an attempt today to repair the broken links between different periods of anticolonial thought, to take a larger historical frame of reference on the coloniality of power, to be wary of European theory idolatry, and to recognize the heterogeneity of European colonialisms.[7]

Dussel's work has been a crucial influence in the decolonial turn by his global framing and his focus on the conquest of the Americas as the critical starting point. His own philosophical training was heavily European, but I would argue that his work on the philosophy of liberation, emerging from the theology of liberation, itself represents an approach indigenous to the western hemisphere. Before turning to his writings on pedagogy I will begin with some remarks on his philosophy of liberation.

Dussel points out that the colonies were a central, causal, and constitutive feature of modernity, including the European Enlightenment, and that the colonized parts of the world actually had some intellectual and political advantages over the myopic tendencies of the Europeans.[8] Turning the tables on Hegel's assessment of the colonies as historically static and philosophically sterile, Dussel presents Hegel's errors — his rush to judgment about peoples and cultures he knew little about and his overly confident characterization of the German epistemological standpoint — as prime evidence that Hegel's own geographical location in fact presented epistemological obstacles, a classic case of what some call the epistemology of ignorance.[9] But on Dussel's view, Hegel is in no way absolved on the grounds of these contextual considerations: Hegel's is a willful ignorance and his invention of developmental modernism served to justify a lack of investigation. Hegel himself believed history and

---

[7] Besides Dussel, readers might consult the work of Rámon Grosfoguel, Walter Mignolo, Sylvia Wynter, Paget Henry, and Lewis Gordon, among others.

[8] Enrique Dussel, *Ethics of Liberation: In the Age of Globalization and Exclusion*, trans. Alejandro A. Vallega, Nelson Maldonado-Torres, Eduardo Mendieta, Yolanda Angulo, and Camilo Pérez Bustillo (Durham: Duke University Press, 2013). This argument is elaborated in the book's introduction.

[9] See, e.g., Shannon Sullivan and Nancy Tuana, eds., *Race and the Epistemologies of Ignorance* (New York: SUNY Press, 2007).

culture to have philosophical relevance, but for him this fact did not support relativism but an absolutist justification of his own epistemological standpoint. It was only because Hegel wrote *from* Europe that he could write *of* Man. A major task Dussel takes up is to show how this idea has been maintained in Western-influenced philosophies from Weber through Habermas.

In contrast, Dussel acknowledges the non-universal nature of his own context of enunciation. Like every other Latin American philosopher since El Inca Garcilaso de la Vega, Dussel has been forced to contemplate how his context is situated with respect to the regime of European truth. Dussel accepts Hegel's view about the relevance of location and the necessity of reading the history of philosophy in light of the history of the world. Hence, historical location is inevitably a part of philosophical thought, and philosophical thought is advanced via a dialectic. But crucially, Dussel drops Hegel's developmentalism and redefines the local in a more global frame. Europeans largely denied that European modernity was dependent on the transnational flows of ideas and goods that colonialism intensified, and instead characterized their Enlightenment as "self-caused," to mimic Aquinas's characterization of God. In contrast, Dussel maintains that modernity has always been a decentralized, global phenomenon. As a result, there is no local that can proclaim itself to be the vanguard. There is only domination and a plethora of global victims. Dussel replaces the Hegelian perspectivism grounded in an imagined developmentalist trajectory of time with a materialist perspectivism grounded in the geography of place, both literal and structural. The world looks differently depending on who is doing the looking.

From his own spatial location (in exile in Mexico since the right-wing military coup in Argentina forced him to leave the country in 1975), Dussel deconstructs not only Hegel's colonial developmentalism but also his central thesis: that the story of human history is the story of the advancement of freedom. Dussel rejects Hegel's claim that freedom is the central criterion that establishes whether progress has been achieved. For Hegel freedom is the central concept for both history and philosophy, since it alone drives the dialectic and explains historical ruptures and motivates the cunning of reason and the ongoing growth of human understanding. The freedom to move, to grow, to expand, to create the conditions for autonomy, and also, we might silently think, the freedom to vanquish anyone who stands in the way. Because, for Hegel, freedom is the story of human history, the development of freedom countermands every other consideration, ethical or otherwise. In contrast, for Dussel the central concept is life, material life. The ultimate ethical criterion is not freedom but the "reproduction or development of the life of each human subject in the community."[10] Systems — whether philosophical, political, or economic — which thwart and inhibit the reproduction or development of material life are invalid.

Yet, in a sense, to value life is to value the creative capacity: human beings being what they are, the nature of life can never coexist with stasis or the cessation of movement and development. Citing the Chilean biologist and philosopher Humberto Maturana, Dussel puts this as follows: "We are a moment of autopoietic life."[11] Hence, the protection of life will protect the capacity to continue the open-ended movements of history. Hegelian freedom, at least in some of its iterations, has served as an alibi for the destruction of life, even whole cultural communities. For Dussel, Hegel doesn't understand freedom. By making freedom more important than material life he in fact diminishes freedom. In Dussel's rendering, the protection of material life will maximize the creative capacity of the species.

Dussel suggests that the struggle of victims (defined as all those excluded from the very ability to maintain and secure their lives[12]) is to discover non-truth, non-validity, and non-efficacy. Echoing Adorno here, Dussel holds that to make sense of the fact that the impoverishment of the majority of the world's people and the imminent danger of eco-suicide are not on the

---

10 Dussel, *Ethics of Liberation*, 128 and 289–90.
11 Ibid., 58.
12 Ibid., 279–84.

agenda of dominant systems of thought, we need to cultivate a skepticism toward the intelligible, the valid, and the true. Only through discovering the fundamental lack in currently dominant systems, processes, and values can the community of victims reach toward creative, reconstructive formulations.

And so, for Dussel, the agenda of a philosophy of liberation must include a commitment to a critique of vanguardism in all forms and an enactment of a democratic epistemology in which the source of knowledge is understood to be communal rather than technocratic and elitist.[13] He argues that the central role in liberation is always played by the excluded and the victims who have proven over and over their capacity for insight and creativity. The social movements, counter-discourses, and reconceived institutions that communities of the activist oppressed continuously create are what drives liberation:

> The *subject of the praxis of* liberation is the living, needy, natural, and thus, cultural subject, and in the last instance the victim, the community of victims, and those who are co-responsibly articulated with it.[14]

Finding non-truth, non-validity, and non-efficacy cannot happen without acknowledging the epistemic resources of everyday existence in the lives of victims, the true agents of ethical criticism and reconstruction.

This brings us to the task of decolonizing the sphere of education. These core elements of the philosophy of liberation — the central focus on material life, the creative capacity of victims, and the need for a democratic epistemology in order to reach the exteriority of the current system — can be discerned in Dussel's writings on education.

For Dussel, what it would mean to decolonize pedagogy, I want to suggest, involves making two major methodological shifts: a shift to a naturalized theoretical approach to education

---

13 Ibid., 240.
14 Ibid., 385.

and a shift from ideal to non-ideal approaches. Though related, these shifts are distinct. A naturalized philosophy of education would base descriptive analysis on the actual practice of teaching as it is embedded in the cross-generational work of community reproduction, while the non-ideal approach then takes real world conditions to craft pedagogical norms or prescriptions. Both of these methodological approaches are enacted in his writings on education.

The naturalized approach Dussel advances begins not with the prescriptive question about what kind of workforce our educational institutions today should be preparing for the future, what assortment of skills our economy needs right now, but with the question of how a given community of adults interacts with a given community of children and youth in material and concrete ways given their different positionality with respect to the temporal dimension of collective life. In other words, the naturalized approach takes the perspective of the most fundamental and material aspect of education: the cross-generational encounter. Dussel calls this the question of the *pedagogic,* as distinct from pedagogy, to distinguish "the science of teaching or learning," or *pedagogy,* from "that part of philosophy that thinks through face-to-face relationships." In this context the face-to-face relationships occur across differences of status but within relationships of care, such as father–son, teacher–disciple, doctor–patient, and politician–citizen. Each of these sorts of relationships defy the expectation of equality, are enacted through difference, and are guided by the dictates of care as well as the material necessity of communal reproduction and regeneration.

Thus the question of the pedagogical begins with the child in a household and concludes with an adult who shares responsibility for their community. The young have a different relationship to the future, and a larger set of needs and vulnerabilities. The encounter between individual teachers and students occurs with these differences of temporality and condition always already in place, affecting the nature of the interaction, its stakes, and its outcome. Dussel reminds us that cross-generational encounters between human beings involve, in the first instance, bodies and breasts, the provision of sustenance, comfort, and safety, and that the face-to-face-encounter between generations always occurs against a backdrop of impassable differences. This does not entail that children are never empowered vis-à-vis adults, but that the temporal differences cannot be set aside as tangential or something that can be transcended.

Dussel's naturalistic language should be read as a feature of his Levinasian-inspired phenomenology. But unlike Emmanuel Levinas, Dussel's naturalism is not paired with decontextualized generalities about the existential grounds for ethics, but with a political analysis of the concrete and material histories of the present. To take a naturalistic view requires an analysis of material realities in all their variation. Thus, for Dussel, the question of cross-generational encounters cannot be approached in terms of global generalities alone, but in relation to actual cultural communities who are attempting to provide sustenance, comfort, and safety as well as ensure their communal regeneration under very specific conditions.

Dussel's approach here parallels a similar move that was made some decades ago in the sub-disciplines of philosophy of science and epistemology, shifting from an attempt to rationally reconstruct the process of justifying theories after the fact to a project of describing how scientists actually pursue their inquiries in the moment, in the laboratory, in the process of collective work.[15] Idealized portrayals of scientific determinations that occluded sociological and non-rational influences were then replaced in this naturalized approach by more accurate characterizations that involved, for example, instances of negotiation. Naturalizing the philosophy of science made it possible to provide better assessments, evaluations, and eventually prescriptions based on actually existing practice. Hence, a naturalized approach considers science not in the idealized terms of "Man's Journey of Discovery," but as consisting of actual research teams

---

15 See, e.g., Ronald N. Giere, "Naturalized Philosophy of Science," *Routledge Encyclopedia of Philosophy*, https://www.rep.routledge.com/articles/naturalized-philosophy-of-science.

created through the vagaries of racist and sexist institutions controlled by capital interests with quite specific practical aims. Science can then be seen for what it is, grounded in human need and both enabled and challenged by every social dynamic in its context, including political and economic ones.

Thus I suggest first of all that we read Dussel as performing a similar function by naturalizing philosophy of education, and moving theory into the temporal, generational reality of human social reproductions under quite specific conditions. On the one hand, this brings to the fore the general condition of community survival and continuation as the constituting motive of pedagogical practice, while on the other it allows for a re-contextualization of specific schoolrooms in specific social moments, with actual faculties created through the vagaries of hierarchical social structures rather than imagined in their ideal state. In other words, the naturalistic frame is what produces both Dussel's expansive outlook on education as well as his focus on actual practices within contexts of domination. The general charge of continuity must be adduced within actually existing conditions.

The second methodological shift Dussel is making is the move to non-ideal theory. To repeat what I said earlier, this move is related yet distinct from the naturalistic move. The point of a naturalized philosophy of education is to argue that descriptive analysis should be based in the practices embedded in the cross-generational work of community reproduction. The point of the non-ideal approach is primarily prescriptive, taking real world conditions in local contexts to craft pedagogical prescriptions.[16] This is a recent push in social theory and philosophy, coming particularly from a number of critical race philosophers and feminists. The tradition of European political philosophy has been shaped by texts such as Plato's *Republic*, Hobbes's *Leviathan*, Thomas More's *Utopia*, and John Rawls's *Theory of Justice*, all of which put forth ideals out of imagined

---

16 See Charles Mills, "'Ideal Theory' as Ideology," *Hypatia* 20, no. 3 (2005): 165–84.

generic thought experiments unconstrained by sociological realities. One must have such decontextualized ideals, it has been argued, before one can identify specific shortcomings in a current society or justify projects for redress. The ideal precedes the non-ideal. Against this, non-ideal theorists hold that the work of developing political and ethical norms requires before anything else an assessment of real world, non-ideal conditions. Norms of practice will emerge from an understanding of the obstacles we encounter now, the challenges we face in this context. This means our norms are no longer universal, timeless, generic.

Dussel's anti-pedagogy is grounded in an awareness of poverty and colonialism, racism and sexism, and new forms of oppressions that are constantly articulated in social movements. In Dussel's view, the activist oppressed are not in need of ideal theory crafted through the thought experiments of elites to mount campaigns or develop new theory.

In *Emile, or on Education,* Jean-Jacques Rousseau himself offered a pedagogy of liberation grounded in the European Enlightenment ideals of a universal culture that would nurture the creative capacity of free minds and noble hearts. This idea of a universal culture legitimated the ideal-theory approach to the philosophy of education, with no need for contextually specific norms. Dussel turns to Rousseau repeatedly as a foil, a contrast, an exemplary mistake. His principal criticism is that the ideal of universal culture that Rousseau advocates for trades on the destruction of actually existing cultures. And so Rousseau instructs the teacher that it makes no difference whether the child has a father or mother. In any case, their particular genealogy has no bearing on the universal culture to which they should assimilate. The condition of the child's actually existing cultural community is irrelevant. Rousseau's utopian vision of a universal culture is thus no amalgamation or sublation of what exists and has existed; it is a substitution based on erasure. The child's own culture of origin (or their people's culture) can be justifiably ignored.

Given this overall orientation, the teacher is then positioned not as the generational equivalent of the parent, or as the parent's partner or collaborator in pursuing the cross-generational work of survival. Rather, in Rousseau's approach the teacher is the anti-parent, the pure, unsituated representative of universal or transcendental value pitted against the particular way of life of the child's own community.

Educators have often been presented as *correctives* to community conventions in this way and hence as oppositional to the other influences being exerted on children and youth, especially those coming from parents and communities. Such teachers are then understandably eyed with suspicion by the community and with defensiveness or outright antagonism by the parent. For impoverished parents with little formal education, this may be a competition in which they lack the confidence to engage, with no hope to win. Rousseau insists that the student should observe a unilinear command structure, obeying *only* the teacher. His is a pedagogy that commands rather than inspires. To the extent it is followed without challenge, Dussel holds that it cannot but ensure the further subordination of oppressed communities, not their survival, but their eradication. It is ideal theory enacting colonization and oppression.

As an alternative, Dussel argues for an "anti-Emile" that would reverse the power relations presented by Rousseau. In reality, the teacher is never a representative of universal culture coming to enlighten with a prior grasp on the truth. In real-world contexts today such narratives only provide cover for pedagogies that are Eurocentric and colonizing. The teacher and the parent are in actuality correlative in their generational relationship to the child and youth. Both are involved in the process of the cross-generational encounter. In Rousseau's view, the parent represents stasis, while the teacher represents advance, as if only the teacher–student relation has a temporal orientation toward the future. But both are engaged in a face-to-face relation to students/children as the harbingers of a future.

Dussel departs from Rousseau's authoritarianism in the name of enlightenment to insist on the relationality of the teacher–student and parent–child encounter. Because it is always a relationality across temporal distance, it resists the stasis that worries Rousseau and contains inherently creative possibilities. This temporal distance makes the child or youth an "Other": "The child cannot be a possibility for the parents because his being is not founded in their project, rather it transcends them." The child reaches "beyond the most extreme possibility of [the parents'] world," constituting "another world, another human."

Moreover, teachers are also in material relations with their students. The teacher cannot imagine himself, as Rousseau would have it, as an

> aseptic preceptor, identified with the gods nor nature. The teacher is such, of a certain sex, a determined moment, a community and State, a nation, a social class, an era of humanity, with its doctrines and theories. [...] He therefore does not have the right to present himself before the disciple as if he had all the rights, and especially the right to be obeyed without limit, like the preceptor in Emile.

Hence, the teacher–student relation is a temporal relation between two materially specific beings, and is therefore subject to the ethics of self/Other relations. The cross-generational encounter can neither be a one-way process of imparting Truth, nor one that abdicates the responsibility of the older generation or denies their influence. It must evolve a relationship through the praxis of mutual listening, what he calls the *conditio sine qua non* of *agapē* or moral love.

Such mutuality is negated and rendered impossible by Rousseau's commandist pedagogy that mistrusts the child, as well as the parents and their community, rendering impossible a praxis of dialogue and mediation. Yet for Dussel, the role of the teacher is far from passive, but also involves active intervention. How, then, is the praxis of mutual listening coordinated with — enabling of — intervention on his account?

Consider the real-world context of cross-generational engagements with students from subordinated communities that face colonialism. In these scenarios, teachers are generally hired to teach the "truths" of the current system, with the system's self-legitimation implicitly (or sometimes explicitly) integrated into a curriculum and practice designed to impart the belief that the current social order is "natural, eternal, and sacred," the best of all possible worlds. Yet, the higher or superordinate task of the teacher is a perpetual striving to discern truth, and not to simply parrot existing regimes of accepted doxa. In the case of relating to a subordinated student sitting in a colonized classroom, this will necessarily involve constructing an *exteriority* to the system, Dussel argues. Such an exteriority provides an outlook upon which the current situation in which the student is positioned can be rendered subject first to observation and then to evaluative analysis.

Constructing an exteriority will then involve what Dussel has called "analectical reasoning," or the reasoning that reaches beyond the simple dialectics of response and reaction to a space on the far side of what is intelligible within the terms of the current thought and practice. Subordination itself can be rendered almost invisible within an orientation such as Rousseau's that portrays commandist education as the gift of enlightenment rather than the destruction of difference and the threat to a community's survival. To animate the students' own critical faculties in such a situation requires reaching beyond the sphere of the currently imaginable, reaching toward an exteriority in which the child or youth is conceptualized as coming from a particular culture with something to offer, in which the child or youth is seen as having the capacity to think creatively and not simply obey. Hence, the teacher must *actively* intervene in order to reveal the exteriority that lies outside of colonizing curriculum for the analectical reasoning in which, then, mutual listening between student and teacher can occur.

In this sense, the child becomes an anti-Emile. Dussel writes that it is "Malinche's child who says [w]e are not orphans. Let us simply recognize our real and humble origins." Where Rousseau proposes to transform the student into someone capable of transcending their humble origins, Dussel insists, with Jose Martí, Gustavo Guttierez, Octavio Paz, José Carlos Mariátegui, and others in this tradition that those origins neither can, nor should be, denied or denigrated. When young radical activists in colonized communities find it impossible to identify with the *imago patris* or State or Patriarch in Power, this is continually misread as a manifestation of Freudian Oedipalism or the inevitability of generational revolt. Such frames obscure the contextual conditions of resistance. For Dussel, resistance in colonial contexts is a claiming of exteriority, a decolonial consciousness.

Dussel reminds us that, originally, indigenous teachers were also doctors, lawyers, psychiatrists, artists, and priests. That is, they performed a variety of roles in communities and with the young, including protecting, advocating for, adjudicating, analyzing, serving, and inculcating into religious life. There was no posture of neutrality or of being the transcendent representative of a universal that existed beyond communal life. Rather than passive servants, they were *tlamatines,* or wisdom leaders.

How does a teacher enable a student to imagine the impossible? The first task must be to address the teacher's own imaginary representations of the epistemic condition of the student. If the teacher imagines the child as a *tabula rasa,* as the modern Europeans did, or, conversely, imagines the task of teaching as a process of animating the child's existing memory, as the Ancient Greeks did, a pedagogy of liberation will be beyond reach. Neither erasure of the child's past nor mere repetitive reinscription of that past correctly represents the cross-generational relation in which the student is recognized as an agential subject. If, on the other hand, the teacher–student relation is correctly understood as an encounter between subjects, then students must be conceptualized as active epistemic agents, neither empty vessels nor merely the unthinking stewards of prior cultural knowledge. Dussel describes the pedagogy that can emerge from a cross-generational relation in which students are recognized as epistemic subjects as a "creative revelation." He says,

> the teacher cannot simply deposit a certain amount of knowledge as acquisitions […], rather he must transmit what is acquired, but from the existential situation of the student and from the way in which his creative revelation arrives to

confound itself with the proper problematizing invention of the student.

This type of "transmission" is what he calls the pedagogical analectic.

In reality, the universal culture that educational institutions imagine themselves to be imparting to students still today emerges without imaginative work since it is a mirror of elite culture. Dussel says "[t]he praxis of pedagogical domination is based on the postulate that there is no other possible speech than that which expresses the meaning of the established world." In this case the teacher–father–state is in a relation of domination, not dialogue, with the student–child–community, as Freire argued.[17] In the colonial context this means that only the cultural national elite is accorded the role of active subject. To the extent creative intelligence is nurtured, it is only that creativity conformable to the current system's needs and goals.

Decolonial approaches to pedagogy have rightfully insisted that colonized cultures have rich resources of knowledge which should be acknowledged in the curriculum. This can lead to the concern that a decolonial approach is mainly intended to conserve existing conventions of thought and practice in subjugated communities and are thus counterposed to critique and transformation. Dussel's writings on pedagogy offer an answer to this concern.

To decolonize pedagogy, for Dussel, is not about conserving intact any system or culture as it exists today, but about recognizing the analectical need to think exteriority in order to enable a critical analysis of existing doxa. Only in this way can what he calls "ontological novelty" be interjected into the system, beyond what is today the true, the valid, and the efficacious. But constructing exteriority requires dialogue, a reaching across of the generational chasm, and thus an ethics of relationality that acknowledges the full historical condition and materiality of all participants. For this, teachers need a collaborative approach

---

[17] See Dussel's discussion of Freire in Dussel, *Ethics of Liberation*, 311–20.

that recognizes their own need to learn about the child or student's actual reality. The teacher is not pitted in perpetual opposition to the subordinated communities of their students, but to the national cultures of empire that incapacitate material life and ethical relationships of all sorts. For this the teacher may indeed run the risk of persecution and exile.

— Linda Martín Alcoff
Professor of Philosophy, Hunter College

Translators' Preface

Luis José González, editor of the short standalone volume *La Pedagogica Latinoamericana* by Enrique Dussel (the title of which we have rendered, at Dussel's suggestion, *Pedagogics of Liberation: A Latin American Philosophy of Education*) introduced readers to the book by noting that Dusselian discourse is peculiar. It takes a little getting used to. Once one gets used to it, though, the terms are powerful contributions to philosophy of education, Latin American studies, and the humanities in general. We would like to use this short Translators' Introduction as a kind of "dis-claimer," to play on Emmanuel Levinas's style of breaking words into their etymological parts with a hyphen when calling new attention to their meaning. Throughout the book, many words and terms may seem unfamiliar to readers. However, listening to the voice of these words is exactly the kind of exercise the book's argument requires. We have attempted to stay true to this challenge in our translation.

Take the title of the work and its flagship concept, for example. "Pedagogics," as Dussel told us when he generously answered our questions about the translation, should be considered as a type of philosophical inquiry alongside ethics, economics, and politics. Each of these words takes as its root a Greek term, makes it an English compound adjective-noun ("ethic"[1]), and then denotes a type of inquiry by turning the adjective-noun into a plural ("ethics"). The same goes for the Greek *paidagogos* in Dussel's lexicon, or *pedagogica* in the Spanish. Rendering this in English, we get a compound adjective-noun (pedagogic) and then a plural version of that term (pedagogics) to denote the corresponding philosophical field of inquiry. Reading pedagogics should be like reading the word ethics, or the other fields of inquiry just mentioned.

Though this usage of "pedagogics" is something of a neologism, it makes good sense given the scope of Dussel's inquiry. As he says in the opening lines of the "Preliminary Words": "pedagogics must not be confused with pedagogy." Pedagogy refers to the science of teaching and learning, while pedagogics "is that part of philosophy which considers face-to-face relationships." Drawing from French philosopher Emmanuel Levinas, Dussel examines the dominating and liberating features of intimate, concrete, and observable interactions between different kinds of people who have face-to-face relationships, specifically where there may be an inequality of knowledge and a responsibility to guide, teach, learn, care, or study: teacher–student, politician–citizen, doctor–patient, philosopher–nonphilosopher, and others. Those occupying a potentially superior position in these face-to-face relationships (teachers, politicians, doctors, philosophers) have a clear choice for Dussel when it comes to their pedagogics. They are either open to hearing the voice of the Other, disrupting their sense of what is and should be by a newness beyond what they know; or they will try to communicate and instruct their sense of what is and should be (which Dussel, in a Latin American context, associates with dominant cultures) to the *tabulae rasae* in their charge. Dussel calls that sense of what is and should be *lo Mismo*, another term which comes from Levinas. The French in Levinas is *le Même,* and we have translated

---

[1] "Ethic" is an English rendering of *ethikē*, a Greek word used in phrases like *ethikē philosophia,* which names the realm of philosophical thinking devoted to morality, customs, and behavior.

Dussel's *lo Mismo* as "the Same."[2] As mentioned at the outset, another Levinasian trait are words with hyphens breaking apart their etymological composites. Dussel follows him in this as well. Dis-tinct, pro-ject, meta-physics, and others pepper the text. The hyphens focus a new attention on the words themselves.

Dussel's lexicon is not just Levinasian, however. It is an eclectic tapestry which includes Latin American history, literature, and philosophy, as well as the more Eurocentric traditions of Ancient Greek philosophy, Thomist theology, modern Enlightenment philosophy, analytic philosophy of language, Marxism, psychoanalysis (Freudian, Kleinian, evolutionary psychology, neuroscience), phenomenology (Sartrian, Heideggerian, Husserlian, Hegelian), critical theory (Frankfurt School, Habermasian), and linguistics. We have done our best with the translations of particular terms given our experience with these diverse traditions, which is comparatively limited compared to Dussel's fluency in them. We have rendered terms like "introjection" in their original form, for example. This particular word comes from psychoanalysis, which Dussel understands (close to Freud's usage) as a process of subjectivation where a person incorporates contents from society into their sense of self.

Many of the passages Dussel cites from the Latin American tradition, particularly in the first chapters, were new to us. We found as many previously existing English translations as we could and did our best translating those we could not find.[3] The book's footnotes are an intellectual achievement on their own, and we encourage readers to seek out the texts Dussel cites and consult them. They form a kind of philosophical bibliography

---

2 The translators of Dussel's *Ethics of Liberation* have rendered it as "the 'Same,'" leaving the "the" out of the quotation marks. We have chosen to leave it in since Dussel includes the *lo*. Interestingly, English translations of Levinas sometimes render *le Même* as "the same," uncapitalized. Dussel was clear that it should be capitalized in his usage. See Enrique Dussel, *Ethics of Liberation: In the Age of Globalization and Exclusion,* trans. Alejandro A. Vallega, Nelson Maldonado-Torres, Eduardo Mendieta, Yolanda Angulo, and Camilo Pérez Bustillo (Durham: Duke University Press, 2013).

3 Many thanks to Rafael Vizcaino in particular for helping us find some of these translations.

for Dussel's oeuvre as it applies to education. As part of our commitment to Latin American philosophy of education, we have rendered the titles of Spanish texts into English, but have left French and German texts in their original languages.

This short book we have titled *Pedagogics of Liberation: A Latin American Philosophy of Education* is part of the larger project called *Para una Ética de la Liberación Latinoamericana*. This larger book, or "work" as Dussel refers to it in the Preliminary Words, is composed of several "books," published in multiple volumes by several publishers in at least two languages over more than a decade. Kaleidescopic and genre-defying in its organization, one way to think about *Para una Ética de la Liberación Latinoamericana* is as a series of published volumes. Yet this quickly becomes inadequate for capturing the fullness of the work. The first two volumes of *Para una Ética de la Liberación Latinoamericana* appeared in 1973 as *Para una Ética de la Liberación Latinoamericana, Tomo I and Tomo II*.[4] Dussel then published a short book on pedagogics as a standalone volume in 1980.[5] It is this short book which we have translated.

However, the same "book" may be found, two years later, as the second half of a third "book" (or published volume) of *Para una Ética de la Liberación Latinoamericana,* published in Portuguese, which includes an Erotica along with the Pedagogica.[6] It can therefore be difficult to talk about "books" in this context, given that some books in the series occur as parts of other books, and some books are volumes containing multiple books.

Dussel has an ingenious way of solving this problem, however. Another way of thinking about *Para una Ética de la Liberación Latinoamericana* is as a single book containing at least

---

4   Enrique Dussel, *Para una Ética de la Liberación Latinoamericana, Tomo I* (Buenos Aires: Siglo Veintiuno, 1973) and Enrique Dussel, *Para una Ética de la Liberación Latinoamericana, Tomo II* (Buenos Aires: Siglo Veintiuno, 1973).

5   Enrique Dussel, *La Pedagogica Latinoamericana* (Bogotá: Editorial Nueva America, 1980).

6   Enrique Dussel, *Para uma Ética da Libertação Latino-americana III: Erótica e Pedagógica* (São Paulo: Edições Loyola-UNIMEP, 1982).

eight chapters and fifty-three sections, together articulating an expansive philosophy of social life from a liberation perspective, focusing on (but certainly not limited to) the Latin American experience. In this schema, the chapters are the following:

1. Fundamental Ontology (sections 1–6)
2. Ontics (sections 7–12)
3. Exteriority of the Other (sections 13–19)
4. Fundamental Eticity (sections 20–25)
5. Morality of "Praxis" (sections 26–31)
6. Ethical Methods (sections 32–39)
7. Erotics (sections 40–47)
8. Pedagogics (sections 48–53)

Each of these chapters is an aspect of the ethic of Latin American liberation: the fundamental ontology of liberation, the ontics of liberation, etc. (We believe this is why Dussel encouraged us to name the short book you read now *Pedagogics of Liberation*.) According to this schema, the pedagogics of liberation we have translated is the eighth chapter of *Para una Ética de la Liberación Latinoamericana,* containing sections 48–53. We have also included section 18 from Chapter III as a sort of "first chapter," since it is in section 18 where Dussel first introduced the concept of pedagogics in *Para una Ética de la Liberación Latinoamericana.*

Dussel makes reference to the other sections of *Para una Ética de la Liberación Latinoamericana* throughout this translation. Due to the complexity of the work itself, we have simplified references to *Para una Ética de la Liberación Latinoamericana* by making reference only to the chapters and sections, in some cases noting page numbers. To find what Dussel is citing, readers can find the section number in the above list and its corresponding published volume through the citations in the footnote 4.

This chapter–section schema for understanding *Para una Ética de la Liberación Latinoamericana,* the larger work for which this little book was written, is why we have numbered the sections of this edition you read now in the seemingly strange way we have: starting with section 18, then skipping to 48–53.

First, we have done this to preserve a sense of the immensity of *Para una Ética de la Liberación Latinoamericana*. Reading this book is like visiting one street in a major global city and we wanted to make that apparent in its presentation. Second, we want to highlight the gaping hole in English-language Dusselian studies: our translation of *La Pedagogica Latinoamericana* appears to be the first English translation of any of the chapters or sections of *Para una Ética de la Liberación Latinoamericana*. The preceding seven chapters and forty-seven sections remain unavailable in English, and by numbering the chapters of this book according to Dussel's intended schema, we gesture to other students of Dussel — ask them, in a way — to start translating the others. Dussel has given his readers the gift of a helpful online archive of his published writings, making hundreds of his books available for free download as PDF files.[7] We recommend checking them out.

While translating this book's arguments and understanding them in the context of their larger intellectual production was difficult, rendering its references and citation apparatus were particular challenges. We have used the Chicago Manual of Style construction similar to that found in the journal *Educational Theory* for our citation approach. This differs from Dussel's citation approach in the original work, which was wide-ranging across languages, translations, and editions.

Part of this translation's contribution is to make visible and available the variety of sources Dussel used to produce his pedagogics of liberation. Since the book is part of our ongoing study of Latin American philosophy of education, we have translated all Spanish language titles into English. When such a citation occurs we maintain the Spanish title and follow it with an English translation of the title in brackets, followed by its original Spanish publishing information. Such bracketed English translations do not occur where there are already existing English

---

7   Enrique Dussel, "Libros," http://enriquedussel.com/Libros_ED.html.

translations of the works. Where we were able to find an English translation of a text, we provide the bibliographic information for that text after the original citation, preceded by the word "English: ...". Any succeeding reference to the book refers to the English text. German, French, Latin, and Greek textual citations we leave in their original languages and editions.

Conforming to *Educational Theory*'s style, all bibliographic information can be found in the footnotes. We have done our best to conform to a singular citational construction, though in some cases we could not find all bibliographic information needed to satisfy those requirements (which we indicate to readers where necessary).

We feel incredibly excited and honored to have translated this book. We think it contains a distinctly Latin American and original philosophy of education that will be critically useful to scholars and practitioners interested in thinking about teaching, learning, and studying. *Pedagogics of Liberation: A Latin American Philosophy of Education* also makes an important contribution to the translation of Dussel's prolific writings, many of which — we are sad to say — are not yet available in English.

In closing, we would like to thank Vincent W.J. van Gerven Oei and Eileen Joy at Punctum for their rigor, patience, and encouragement in this project (and Arthur J. Russell for connecting us to them). We also want to acknowledge those who helped in the editing, translating, citation-finding, and other labors which birthed this translation, specifically Jason T. Wozniak, Rafael Vizcaino, Christopher Casuccio, Antonio Medina-Rivera, and Tomas Rocha.

— David I. Backer,
Assistant Professor of Education,
West Chester University of Pennsylvania, USA

— Cecilia Diego
Co-creator Esto no es una escuela,
Mexico City, Mexico

Preface to the English Edition

This pedagogics (a *philosophical* text, not a pedagogical or empirical text) is part of a much more extensive work written over a period of five semesters between 1970 and 1975. It was in 1975 that I was fired from the Universidad Nacional de Cuyo in Argentina, due to a military dictatorship that officially took power in 1976 in my *patria chica* (my *patria grande* being Latin America, the Caribbean, and the *latinos* in the United States). 1975 was also the year I began my exile in Mexico. Having discovered that my book *The Ethics of Liberation*[1] had been quite abstract, addressing fundamental principles in the first two volumes, which gave it the initial mark of a categorical-theoretical framework, I developed the next four parts to give the book a more concrete orientation: the erotics (which today we would associate with questions about gender and the liberation of women and other consequences of gender), the pedagogics (which is the third volume of the *Ethics,* and is comprised of this book in English translation, covering the liberation of children, young people,

---

1 Enrique Dussel, *Ethics of Liberation: In the Age of Globalization and Exclusion*, trans. Alejandro A. Vallega, Nelson Maldonado-Torres, Eduardo Mendieta, Yolanda Angulo, and Camilo Pérez Bustillo (Durham: Duke University Press, 2013).

and the people's culture), the politics (liberation of brothers, sisters, and friends), and three further books on anti-fetishism (addressing the question of reverence and sacrilege viz. practical totalities).

Pedagogics of Liberation, which you hold in your hands, is therefore part of a wide-ranging philosophical inquiry that makes certain presuppositions. This *Pedagogics* must be situated within the totality of that larger critical project.

Linda Martín Alcoff's introduction to this volume offers many explanations. I would therefore like to use this Prologue to position this text, which is almost forty years old, on the horizon of the Global South.

This short book gives voice to many discoveries that were developed over the years preceding it, but its principal and original insight is to consider the question of pedagogics in a geopolitical, cultural, and global context. More specifically, its aim is to think through the universal pretensions of Eurocentric pedagogics (*the universality claim of Eurocentrism*), as well as those of North America, thereby reclaiming the colonial (or neocolonial) periphery's right to its proper Latin American history — a history whose particularity they did not know because of modernity's domination. Here we see "the provincialization" of the United States and Europe. In other words, without asking the question itself yet, the book is about the pedagogical foundations of *epistemological decolonization,* which occupies us today. And I would alert readers that in 1973, when I was drafting this very manuscript, the project to decolonize knowledge was articulated, before Edward Said did so in literature with his *Orientalism,* and before those in subaltern studies, like Rajanit Guha, did so for history in India, or before J.F. Lyotard's Eurocentric postmodernism was developed.[2]

---

[2] Edward W. Said, *Orientalism* (New York: Vintage, 1979); Ranajit Guha and Gayatri Chakravorty Spivak, eds., *Selected Subaltern Studies* (Oxford: Oxford University Press, 1988); Jean-François Lyotard, *The Postmodern Condition: A Report on Knowledge,* trans. Geoffrey Bennington and Brian Massumi (Minneapolis: University of Minnesota Press, 1984).

We would like to note also that this translation has conserved a certain masculine patriarchy in its language, which was present in the Spanish text as well. The original text was neither attentive to the use of words like *man, father, son, him,* etc., nor to those words referring to women, like *woman, mother, daughter, her,* etc. Over time, we have found that others words are more appropriate, like *human being, person, parents,* etc. I was aware then of *patriarchal machismo* and also of a nascent feminism (to which I dedicated the first part of the *Ethics* in those years), but I did not yet know, at that time, how to overcome the problem linguistically.

I have elaborated on the pedagogics of liberation in a number of other books, but I hope that this English translation initiates a fruitful dialogue in philosophy of education horizontally, South — South (between and among those in Latin America, Africa, the Muslim world, India, Southeast Asia and China) as well as globally, South-North (of those aforementioned cultures with Europe, the United States, Russia, etc.). I hope it will help to achieve a transmodern culture where intercultural dialogue can educate a new generation, and create a pluri-versal worldliness (not Eurocentrically uni-versal), one that is epistemologically decolonized: in a word, a culture that respects the existing distinction of the diversity within every community of Humanity.

— Enrique Dussel
Professor Emeritus,
Department of Philosophy, UAM Iztapalapa
Coyoacan, Mexico Tenochtitlan, 2017

PEDAGOGICS OF LIBERATION

PEDAGOGICS OF LIBERATION

PEDAGOGICS OF LIBERATION

PEDAGOGICS OF LIBERATION

PEDAGOGICS OF LIBERATION

Youth does not ask. It demands the recognition of its right to exteriorize its own thinking.

— Córdoba Manifesto of 1918

There was a breathing spell. The students, full of hope, gathered for a meeting—not a demonstration—in the Plaza of Tlatelolco on the second of October. At the end of the meeting, when those attending it were about to leave, the plaza was surrounded by the army and the killing began. A few hours later it was all over. How many died? The Guardian, after a careful investigation, considered the most probable: 325[...]. The second of October, 1968, put an end to the student movement[...]. It was an instinctive repetition that took the form of an expiatory ritual.

— Octavio Paz, *Posdata*

Preliminary Words

Pedagogics of Liberation continues the work already underway in *Para una Ética de la Liberación Latinoamericana*. Man is now the father. Woman, the mother. The *new one* (the Other) is now the child.

Pedagogics must not be confused with pedagogy. The latter is the science of teaching or learning. Pedagogics, on the other hand, is the part of philosophy (along with ethics, politics, and economics) which considers face-to-face relationships: the parent–child, teacher–student, doctor–patient, philosopher–nonphilosopher, politician–citizen, etc. Pedagogics as we intend it here has a greater significance than pedagogy, covering all types of "discipline" (what is received from another) existing in opposition to "invention" (what is discovered on one's own). Furthermore, the study of pedagogics is unique because it is the point of convergence and mutual passage between the erotic and the political — which we will address in the next sections of *Para una Ética de la Liberación Latinoamericana*. Basically, pedagogics begins with the child of the erotic household and concludes with the adult of political society. Yet in another way, it begins with the child in the pedagogical-political institution (culture, school, etc.) and concludes with a man or woman formed for a fruitful erotic life. Therefore, pedagogics clearly begins and ends

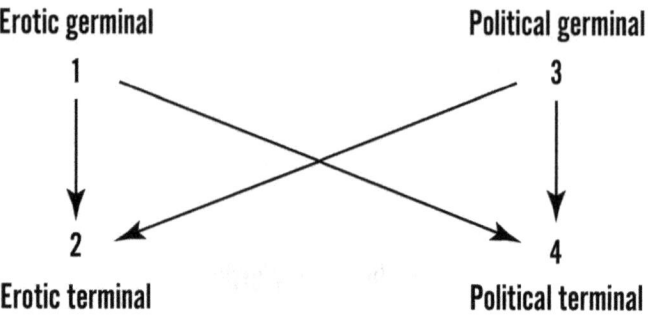

Figure 1. The pedagogical as convergence of the erotic and the political.

in the same erotics (of the child to the parents in the domain of the home) and the same politics (of the child to the teacher or pedagogue in the domain of the school). This four-part dimensionality complicates the explanation of this particular chapter of the larger work, but the nature of pedagogics demands such an explanation.

As stated above (Figure 1), the son or daughter born in the family (1) is educated so that one day they become a father or mother (2) and at the same time become an adult citizen (4). Children in political-pedagogical institutions (3) are disciplined to one day be responsible for the community (4) or adults at the erotic level (2). Thus, in the sections that follow, we will always begin with the pedagogical-erotic and pass to the pedagogical-political (though it would be possible to take the inverse path: from the pedagogical-political to the erotic). We will make this move whether the subject under consideration is *symbolism and pedagogics* (section 48), the starting point of all our situated Latin American reflections, or in the interpretation of *ontology and pedagogics* (section 49) and in its overarching *meta-physic* (section 50). In the same way, the problematic of *economy and pedagogics* (section 51) will begin with erotic economy and culminate in political economy, since a pedagogics of economy depends on the family as much as the State or culture. We will also, in the last two sections, address *a pedagogics of liberation* (sections 52 and 53), and take into consideration the aforementioned bipolarity of educational phenomena.

In this complicated chapter of the larger *Para una Ética de la Liberación Latinoamericana,* then, in addition to addressing traditional questions of evolutionary psychology or child psychoanalysis from birth to adulthood, and the problems already raised by pedagogics in its multiple aspects, we must also discuss childhood, ideology, culture, and all this in the context of dependency and liberation. We will, in other words, expound an *anti-pedagogy*.[1]

---

1 The concept of pedagogics is introduced in section 18 of *Para una Ética de la Liberación Latinoamericana*. See "Translators' Preface" for details.

18

"The Other" as the Face of Pedagogics[1]

A child is born. A real novelty, the chosen and unique "Other." The child is thrown into his or her world. That is all there is. Nobody asks for the child's thoughts on the possibility of existing (an absurd question, one which occupied Sartre for so long). This would require the child to be present before conception. Rather, we hail from paternal fecundity. We are not from a physical time; nor are we, at least (and originally), from temporality (since temporality is ontological and is *itself* a moment of the pro-created[2] child). Rather we are from a unique, non-transferable, personal time. This time is the time of life (which might be documented in a biography). This time is a time of personal destiny: a messianic time (if "messianism" is understood as the time of waiting during which the child will accomplish his alterative pro-ject). There is no more profound waiting than the waiting of letting-be (*Gelassenheit*); letting-be a *new* history, embodied in the child, a history which is just beginning. This history is

---

1 Translator: The following is section 18 of chapter III of Enrique Dussel, *Para una Ética de la Liberación Latinoamericana*. See "Translators' Preface" for details.

2 Translator: Here is the first instance of Dussel's Levinasian use of hyphenation. One can see it also in the following phrases in this section: "alterative pro-ject," "dis-tinct" and "dif-ference."

"new" because it is unique; "new" because it is unpredictable; "new" because it is unrepeatable. "The Other," the child, the fruit of fecundity, is liberty-as-creation, pro-creation, recreation but never a return: never repetition, cycle, or memory. Dis-tinct in its origin, it has a vocation to be "the Same" as that which is, which is to say: it has a vocation to be the Other for every other.

Therefore, the child, free and autonomous, the dis-tinct "Other," begins an essentially separate relation in the real constitution *in utero*. This constitution is the origin of its ontological organization: the dis-course with "the Other," pedagogical alterity, from which pro-creation emerges to penetrate the history which precedes it. Pedagogical alterity will accomplish its messianic function *within* this preceding history (*moshiach* comes from the Hebrew for the anointing "oil": "anointed" in our case signifies that every child arrives anointed with his non-transferable, unique, unrepeatable, and authentic destiny). As dis-tinct the child is a *tabula rasa* (the pure possibility of sensing the world, having not yet sensed anything). Thus born poor, and tasked with everything that will be his history and her life. It is in this primal moment of the pro-created, who is not yet fully a creator, that Alterity accomplishes what we could call the meta-physical function, or the ethic of pedagogy. The child (in Greek *pais,* and from now on that which is necessary for any grade of perfection regarding this negative position) must be led by the hand to its proper pro-ject.[3] This "pedagogical time" in a person's life indicates the continuity of human history. "Pedagogical time" also indicates the meta-physical and ethical alterity of humans' being-in-itself. In nine months (from conception until birth) man goes from a unicellular organism to a newborn

---

3 In Greek, *agō* means "to conduce" (pedagogue: the one who conducts the child). *To educate,* however, stems from the Latin: to conduce from the origin, or "educe," "bring to light." For a treatment of the pedagogical matter as we will suggest it here see Paulo Freire, *Pedagogía del Oprimido* (Montevideo: Tierra Nueva, 1970), 247–50; English: Paulo Freire, *The Pedagogy of the Oppressed,* trans. Donald Macedo (New York: Continuum, 2005). For more on the *pro-ject* in the Totality, see what has been said in Dussel, *Para una Ética de la Liberación Latinoamericana, Tomo I,* 52–55.

child uttering his first historical cry (four billion years of life on our planet are travelled ontogenetically *in utero*). From birth until his adult autonomy (never total) man will travel through the "analectic of teaching," traversing the more than two million years he has inhabited the earth. This pedagogical process is neither return, nor repetition. It is neither memory, nor *maieutic*: it is in-novation; it is learning; it is taking "the similar" back to square one and beginning from a dis-tinct starting point. Thus "the similar" becomes *new*. Man is *nothing* with respect to the *sameness* (which is not identical univocality) he receives, and this position constitutes the analogical being of man. "The Other," the newborn, the child will not imitate what others have done but rather re-create what others-in-others have created. His world, a world where he transcends existentially, ontically or mundanely ("the Same"), will begin to grow from "the Other" through cultural, historical, and practical everyday learning. This is the question of the *analectic of teaching*, the human's mode of taking on *tradition*.

The equivocal unity of *eros* which links the minimal alterity of the couple ("the Same") assumes the original dis-tinction between man and woman: that which opens itself again, but this time to the alterity of the child (the new "Other," who, in his origin, is *less* dis-tinct to his parents than his father is dis-tinct to his mother; *more* dis-tinct in relation to his parents than to his siblings). The analectic of parents–child is already a pedagogical relation: the parent is the historical-cultural *anterior* (ontologically and meta-physically); the child is new and has to learn everything (of course, when something has been *understood* and concomitantly *invented*, he will have "some" experience "about" it; an experience which brings about new inventions and understandings that make his world grow). Authentic parents, teachers, journalists, artists, professional politicians, philosophers… hold an analectic position with respect to the children, students, community, non-philosophers, etc. The pedagogical analectic is grounded in a certain paternal and filial love (which is not *eros*, but rather a love in friendship that is equally ambiguous), a superior's love (which can reveal something to the student) of an inferior (and thus the teacher loves the student gratuitously, since the student's love can collapse into mere friendship of pragmatic utility).[4]

In the ontology of Totality (Greek and modern) the dialectic of teaching may be summarized thus (especially in Plato): the teacher, the philosopher, the politician, or parent which comprehends the disciple (or child) as "the Same" must produce the memory of what has been forgotten and made invisible: a remembrance that makes "the Same" acquire actuality through the student's present knowing. Some think that "the Same" can be acquired through the dialectic. Others think it can be acquired through science. Either way, this path to "the Same" results in an understanding of being, the divine, the from-always (the Idea, *ousia*, the Plotinian One). The doctrine of the Rig-Veda and Buddhism also teach "the Same" but with varying ancillary lessons. Modern thought, in terms of subjectivity, casts the disciple as *tabula rasa*, but due to the solipsism unique to its point of departure, this pedagogy is nothing but a leading-out of what is already given in "the noble savage" (Rousseau, Montessori). Modern pedagogy is the originary doctrine of the *ego cogito* (or *the* Hegelian Absolute) that invents, pro-duces, re-presents, or dis-covers everything "from itself" (what Heideggerian *Wiederholung* reiterates in the mundane totality of "the Same" given existentially). The ontology of Totality as pedagogy ultimately results in certain conclusions: for example, that morality is invention (for Sartre), or that the truth is dis-covery (for Heidegger).[5]

In the ontology of Totality, the teacher paradoxically holds both a passive and catalytic position that is not new. Like the Socratic midwife, philosophy is only maieutic. In other words, the task is *already* given, one just needs to give birth to it. Equal-

---

[4] Aristotle saw this very clearly, but with a meaning different from the one we are ascribing it here: Aristotle, *Nicomachean Ethics*, ed. J. Bywater (Oxford: Clarendon Press, 1894), Book IX, 1167b.

[5] See also my Enrique Dussel, *Para una De-strucción de la Historia de la Ética* [*Towards a De-struction of the History of Ethics*] (Mendoza, Argentina: Editorial Ser y Tiempo, 1972), 163–328.

ly, in modern philosophy of education, the teacher must let-be manifestations of the child's spontaneity. Pedagogy, in this sense, merely keeps at bay the influences of foreign elements. In both cases "the Same" (divinely eternal and cosmological for the Greeks; subjective, free, and individual in modernity) brings out the student's actuality from their potentiality. Intrinsically speaking, Alterity, "the Other" as teacher, has nothing to do with that process of bringing out actuality from potentiality (all of this is theoretical, of course, because in praxis the Greek teacher and modern teacher transmitted the historical tradition of their respective communities with an iron-like disciplinary system, without respect for the Other: the disciple as other). The Freudian psychoanalyst fulfills the same function, as does the existential psychiatrist, with their client, and the sick person in privatized medicine. In truth, the Greeks accepted the historical-cultural beliefs of their communities as innate. The moderns believed the ego's invention presumed the Other's continuous learning. The analectic of teaching goes beyond the notion of philosophy-as-maieutic, or as the thinking of what is com-pre-hended.[6] This analectic overcomes the false antinomy between learning as mere memory and all that we invent from the *ego*.

In the meta-physic of the face-to-face, Alterity is essentially and originally constitutive of the world of Totality. Look for examples at the pairing of a teacher's (philosopher's) exteriority and a disciple's (non-philosopher's) exteriority, and the parent confronted with the child ("the Other" that is born dis-tinct). Pedagogics before ontology: "the Other" precedes invention from "the Same." We should not forget however that "the Same" (the child himself as such) proceeds from the Other (parents, a community, and a cultural history with traditions).

---

6 Philosophy, today, will develop a radically innovative, creative, pro-phetic character; it not only thinks about history, it gets in front of history and marks its path. Philosophy will, for us, be praxis in the diverse sense indicated in Dussel, *Para una Ética de la Liberación Latinoamericana*, section 12; it is an analectical praxis (see ibid., section 30).

Searching for an example in universal thought, we find a small book by Augustine of Hippo: *The Teacher*.[7] Augustine, whom Heidegger interpreted with great clarity during the 1919–1920 seminars, deals with the factical experience of Judeo-Christian life, but not with the existential experience thereof in its conceptual formulation. At this point we may say the following: Augustine, starting from an alterative existential position, only had an ontology of the Totality, which led him to an impoverished formulation of alterity (which only a meta-physics of Alterity can formulate, thanks to recent and novel conceptualizations). This impoverished formulation can be perfectly observed in the little tract already mentioned. Augustine begins adequately enough by indicating that the question of pedagogy turns on language and the word: "Augustine: When we speak, what does it seem to you we want to accomplish (*loquimur*)? Adeodatus: So far as it now strikes me, either to teach or to learn (*aut docere, aut discere*)."[8] But immediately Augustine says that we speak only to teach, and that we can definitively teach through memory (*per memorationem*), or as God "wills" it: "from our deepest rational soul, that is what is called inner man."[9] In other words, human Alterity disappears. The Alterity of the face-to-face relationship, which included carnality, even stops expressing God's own "exteriority."

In the thirteenth century, working from a corrected Aristotelian ontology, it is said that

> In one way, natural reason by itself reaches knowledge of unknown things, and this way is called *discovery*, in the other

---

[7] Agustín, "Acerca del maestro," *Obras de San Agustín* (Madrid: BAC Obras filosóficas, 1963), 538–99. English: Augustine, *Against the Academicians and The Teacher*, trans. Peter King (Indianapolis: Hackett Publishing Co., 1995), 94.
[8] Ibid., 94.
[9] Ibid., 95: "[I]n ipsis rationalis animae secretis."

way, when someone else aids the learner's natural reason, and this is called *learning by instruction*.[10]

For this reason, "the teacher or master must have the knowledge which he causes in another explicitly and perfectly."[11] The subject has been indicated, but, at this point, its full historical, cultural, ontological, and meta-physical sense is far from being comprehended.

What has not been clearly demonstrated is that the "invention" (ontological area of "the Same" that develops one's potential) opens itself from the "discipline" (disciplined). Teaching Alterity *creates* in the student, like *revelation* following *nothing* (the teacher as freedom beyond the ontological horizon of "the Same": the student), the "sense" of everything that the child incorporates in his world ("the Same" from "the Other"). But very soon after this student starts to "invent" (pro-ducing from "the Same") his world as a growing being (the seed beginning to send out roots and sprouts…). The pedagogical analectic is established from this moment: "the Other" (the teacher, the parent, the philosopher) must doubly realize "the Same" (the student, the child, the non-philosopher). They must first realize "the Same" radically and with love of justice, because it is a dis-tinct "Other" (free extreme of the spectrum). Simultaneously they must realize "the Same" historically and culturally, and with an analogous love of friendship, because it contains in its making a certain "the Same" of resemblance (as part of the same cultural world: the *familiar* we of the pedagogical, national, and human community).

As dis-tinct, the disciple has a *new* historical pro-ject for being human ("the Other" as real and historical). The teacher cannot simply *deposit* a certain amount of acquired knowledge (the "banking" conception of education, where the only question for

---

10 Tomás de Aquina, "Quaestiones disputatae [Cuestiones disputadas]," *De Magistro* (Torino: Marietti, 1964). English: Thomas Aquinas, *Truth, Vol. II*, trans. James V. McGlynn (Indianapolis: Hackett Publishing Co., 1994), 83.
11 Ibid., 89.

teaching is memory: to *recall*),[12] rather he must transmit what is acquired, but from the existential situation of the student. The teacher must also transmit acquired knowledge from the way in which his *creative revelation* arrives, to confound itself with the student's proper quality of problematizing *invention*. Which is to say, and Heidegger saw this in part, that the teacher must establish a pedagogical analectic that overcomes the apparent dis-tinction between parent–child, teacher–student. This pedagogical analectic is impossible in the ontology of Totality. The teacher professes his word (thus the teacher's authentic word is *pro-phecy*[13]), and his word is the fruit of his authentic invention, as well as the authentic creation from his community ("the Same"), to the Other, his disciple. But in order for his word to be pro-phetic, teacherly, the teacher learns the student's pro-ject concomitantly ("the Same" of the Other: the newness the teacher tends to ignore). The disciple understands the pro-phetic, authentic word of the teacher, "the Other," insofar as the teacher puts "the Same" out there, puts out his world, his pro-ject, in a movement that signifies his authentic realization. At the same time, the student demands an openness from "the Other" that "the Other" (the teacher) has revealed as a creator would reveal it. The ana-lectic, beyond the dia-lectic, teaches that the dia-lectical process moves itself from beyond (*ana-*) the world: from "the Other." The teacher and the disciple always have something to learn (from birth to death), and very soon that same student begins to teach (a small child that teaches his younger brother how to play, for instance) and continues to do so until death. No disciple is purely a disciple; no teacher is purely a teacher. What

---

12 Freire, *Pedagogy of the Oppressed*, 7: "The 'banking' concept of education as an instrument of oppression." It oppresses the given culture and annihilates the Other as other, it makes culture an internal dif-ference of "the Same": the reigning imperial culture; at least the culture of the "system."

13 Pro-phecy comes from the Greek, *pro-* "before," *phēmi* "to speak." The prophet is he who "speaks before" the Other about the "sense" of the *historical present* (this is in the Hebrew tradition): "Hear this, you elders; listen, all who live in the land. Has anything like this ever happened in your days or in the days of your ancestors?" (Joel 1:2).

the teacher learns he also learns from the novelty of the child's pro-ject (youth of the Other that is never equal to the youth of the teacher, because it has originated dis-tinctly in another moment of universal history; because this child is Other metaphysically). Everything the student learns he learns from the Alterity of the teacher, that comes into the student's world from *nowhere* (the teacher's liberty and the anteriority of humanity as global "Other"). All teachers must teach more than what is given simply with anteriority; they must teach how it was reached with a *critical mode*. The teacher does not transmit traditions as traditional, but rather revives the conditions that made it possible to be *new,* unique, creation. Every student teaches his authentic mode and dis-tinct human being, with attention focused on the inventions that he himself ("the Same") contributes to history ("the Other"). These inventions are real. They are neither utopian, dreamy fantasies, nor a house of cards. The reciprocal revelation of teacher and disciple that begins on the part of the elder (teacher, parent) with a just love for the youth (student, child), and that moves within pedagogical friendship of the prophet for his community, can *close itself* equivalently: the teacher can love the student and the latter can love the teacher as "one *of* our own": the sect. This *us* (that in the man–woman relationship is the family, and between Plato and his students could be the Academy) is "the Same." *Closed* friendship will always make the teacher an oppressive teacher and the student a minor, an alienated being. Ultimately this closed friendship would entail a "will to power" and a destruction of the analectic originary of the "personal I of the teacher" in relation the "personal You and Other" of the student. Here we have the psychiatrist exploiting his client and not liberating him from that tutelage which alienates him. In contrast, this position, which is authentically alive, also brings death — the *passage* to another moment where the teacher-as-teacher and the student-as-student, or the parent-as-parent and child-as-child, itself dies as a moment. This moment of death occurs when the child grows and the student learns all the teacher can teach him. It is in this moment the student reaches the plenitude of alterity while still at the minimal level of the initial dis-tinction: brother face-to-face with brother. This is why the teacher as parent will always pronounce "it is good that he (the student, new teacher) grows and that I (as teacher) disappear."[14] This "path" (*hodos* in Greek) is a "method" whose historical-concrete *content* is the *pro-ject of the* unpredictable *Other,* who is always other. The unpredictable other is an impossibility for which one cannot prepare a "lesson" necessitating the con-vergence of the real student and comes to reveal to the teacher the *material* of his course, his dis-course.[15]

To be an authentic teacher is a dangerous, risky job. It entails praxis, an existential commitment, and sometimes puts one's physical life in jeopardy. In the degraded dialectic, the pedagogical Self-Other, the self-educator (parents, society) comes to transform into an impersonal "self" (this is a false tradition; think of the sophist who teaches in the academy as a means for sustenance, according to his theoretical and irreal teachings). The Other-student (child, student of a society massified through opulence or oppression) is also transformed into an impersonal "him," who must be "filled" with "traditional," "safe," and "objective" contents of knowledge. The authentic teacher begins a *new* process, the inverse path to decadence or degradation. He begins a path that destroys the bonds restraining the other's liberty, called from a critical position to recuperate his personal attitude. As such, the teacher is "a new man" and lives that face-to-face relationship in anticipation. He lives in its proximity.

What follows is a figure depicting the above proposals (Figure 2).

---

14 Matthew 11:10.
15 Speaking in terms of the university, pedagogical dialogue takes place in a "seminar," where professor and students study, discuss, and learn together, thinking with one another about certain subjects and texts. University-level "master class" does not justify itself as mere information which is already known (university students have the usual texts for this), but rather must in an actualized manner reach the student anew, where the teacher's methodical thinking creates an irreplaceable revelation.

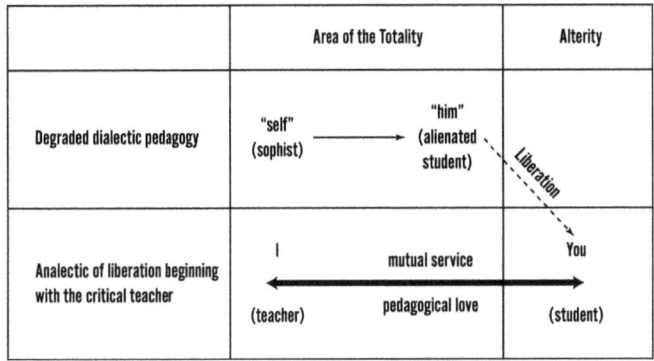

Figure 2. Liberatory position of the teacher in the dialectic of mutual and impersonized reification.

When the teacher comes from the free and autonomous end of the spectrum, as an "I" with the capacity to establish relations irrespective of the self-Other, living in the face-to-face relationship between free beings, he must remain *alone*. The "self" of the collective, the reigning and majoritarian us rushes to kill (professionally, psychologically, physically) that which has pretended to break the dialectic of domination. If the "Self-Teacher" resists fighting with those who have waged war, "the exercise of reason itself,"[16] then he will become surrounded by free men, those "student-Others" that shortly thereafter will be *brothers* in a new historical age. The passage from alienation (when someone stops being "the dis-tinct Other" and goes on to be the internal di-fference of the totalitarian Totality) to liberty, they always initially produce it through pedagogical liberation. All of this must be utilized in the pedagogical method. There are methods that fight against the Totality, pretending to set up a new domination. There are others that negate the closed Totality, trying to open it to Alterity.

---

16 Emmanuel Levinas, *Totalité et infini: essai sur l'extériorité* (The Hague: Nijhoff, 1968), ix.

48

Symbols and Pedagogics

Our hermeneutic reading of pedagogics will begin with an initial suspicion grounded in our knowledge of Latin American reality. The *parent* (the *imago* of the father, and the mother, as well as the teacher, doctor, professional, philosopher, culture, State, etc.) extends his phallocracy in the form of aggression and domination of the child. In other words: filicide. *The death of the child,* the boy, youth itself, those fresh generations, enacted by gerontocracies or bureaucracies, is physical (the front line of an army of human sacrifices), symbolic or ideological. Despite these differences of manifestation, filicide is always a type of alienation, domination, and annihilation of Alterity. Erotic *phallocracy*, mediated by a pedagogics of *filicide,* culminates in political fratricide. These are three aspects of what is today called "the death of God."

In pedagogics, passing from the erotic to the political is continuous. It happens without our noticing. In Latin America, which is still *machista,* the father-as-State opposes the mother-as-culture. Thus:

> I came to Comala because I had been told that my father, a man named Pedro Páramo, lived there. It was my mother who told me [...]: "Don't ask him for anything. Just what's

ours. What he should have given me but never did [...]. Make him pay son, for all those years he put us out of his mind.[1]

The child bears within himself the agonizing bipolarity of father-mother, of violence-culture. The Latin American, a son of Malinche (the Indian that betrayed her culture) and Cortés (father of the conquest and of the virtues of a subordinate State, since, of course Cortés is not a King). The Latin American "does not want to be either an Indian or a Spaniard. Nor does he want to be descended from them. He denies them. And he does not affirm himself as a mixture, but rather as an abstraction: he is a man. He becomes the son of Nothingness. His beginnings are in his own self."[2] This paradoxical position of the child, Latin America itself, emerges because what is *new* can neither accept the more powerful *father's* original domination (first the imperial State and then the neocolonial State, betraying its proper culture), nor can it accept its dominated and violated mother, its culture — who breast-fed its symbols. To discover one's destiny

---

1 Juan Rulfo, *Pedro Páramo* (Mexico: FCE, 1971), 7. English: Juan Rulfo, *Pedro Páramo*, trans. Margaret Sayers Peden, ed. Danny J. Anderson (Austin: University of Texas Press, 2002), 12. On the "nostalgia of the father [*Vatersehnsucht*]," see Sigmund Freud, *The Future of an Illusion* (New York: Broadview Press, 2012). "Little by little I began to build a world around a hope centered on the man called Pedro Páramo, the man who had been my mother's husband. That was why I had come to Comala... 'Pedro Paramo's my father, too,' he said...We're Pedro Páramo's sons alright, but, for all that, our mothers brought us into the world on straw mats. And the real joke of it is that he's the one who carried us to be baptized" (Rulfo, *Pedro Páramo*, 3). The theme of searching for the father is ancient in American thought: "What was my father like? [asked Quetzocoatl], What was his stature? I would like to see his face...! They responded to him: He has died. He was buried far from here" (Angel Garibay, *La Literatura de los Aztecas* [*The Literature of the Aztecs*] [Mexico: J. Moritz, 1970], 24). See also in this same publication "Amonestación del Padre al Hijo" ["A Father's Warning to his Son"], 107.

2 Octavio Paz, *El Laberinto de la Soledad* (Mexico: FCE, 1973), 78–79. English: Octavio Paz, *The Labyrinth of Solitude and Other Writings*, trans. Lysander Kemp, Yara Milos, and Rachel Phillips Belash (New York: Grove Press, 1985). For this pedagogics, we will keep this magnificent chapter, "The Son of La Malinche" (65–88), in mind.

and history one must begin at a distance from the pedagogical, erotic, and political.

> [A]nd a force was invading me through my ears, my pores: the language. Here once more was the language I had talked in my infancy; the language in which I had learned reading and sol-fa... There came back to me, after long forgetting... put away somewhere with a picture of my mother and a blonde lock of my hair cut off when I was six years old.[3]

When the father forgets his wife, it is the same as when the child forgets himself. Forgetting of the mother's being happens in the process of pedagogical domination, enacted by the father and by the Empire. This phallocracy is uxoricide, and therefore also matricide. Filicide, which is a pedagogic of domination itself, originates from this matricide:

> And four days passed and the Sun in the sky was still. All the land was afraid beneath the shadows that dragged on forever. The gods gathered and sought counsel with one another: "Why does it not move?" The Sun was the wounded god transformed into sun, from his throne. The hawk goes and asks: "The gods want to know why you do not move!" And the Sun responded: "You know why? I want human blood! I want them to give me *their children,* I want them to give me *their offspring!*"[4]

---

3 Alejo Carpentier, *Los Pasos Perdidos* (Santiago, Chile: Orbe, 1969), 35. English: Alejo Carpentier, *The Lost Steps,* trans. Harriet de Ónis (Middlesex: Penguin, 1968), 38. We have said that the three women of the text are the three cultures practiced in Latin America: Ruth (imperial culture), Mouche (prostituted culture or high neocolonial elite), Rosario (popular Latin American ancestrality).

4 "El Quinto Sol" ["The Fifth Sun"], in Garibay, *La Literatura de los Aztecas,* 16. The Sun is a masculine mythical moment; the fearful land is the maternal-feminine moment. The child is immolated. See other examples and a modified psychoanalytic interpretation in Arnaldo Rascovsky, *El Filicidio* [*Filicide*] (Buenos Aires: Orión, 1973) — a book of great pedagogical interest. Also see on filicide, Bartolomé de las Casas, *Apologética Historia* [*His-*

This passage describes a pre-Oedipal situation in pre-Hispanic thought because Huitzilopochtli, the Sun, was a small god (the son) immolated by other gods in order to give him sustenance (being sun, as he is). Huitzilopochtil then demands the immolation of all sons everywhere. This is filicide because the son, as child, is positioned between father and mother. His Oedipal hatred of the father arises from this positioning between his parents.

Men have had sons since the beginning, even those primitive "men of wood" of the *Quiché* mythology:

> They existed and multiplied; they had daughters, they had sons, these wooden figures; but they did not have souls, nor minds, they did not remember their Creator, their Maker; they walked on all fours, aimlessly [...]. These were the first men who existed in great numbers on the face of the earth. Immediately the wooden figures were annihilated, destroyed, broken up, and killed.[5]

Progeny is novelty, renovation of the aged, perpetuation and eternity. The world is renewed with the child, with the "new year," with accompanying rites of initiation.[6] But the ontological novelty of the new must introject the current system (which is why it is a child's blood that is sacrificed to conserve the life of the cosmos). Therefore "later our mothers were told, and commanded: 'Go, my sons, my daughters, your obligations will be

---

tory of the Indies] (Madrid: Bailly, Bailliere e hijos, 1909); José de Acosta, "Historia Natural y Moral de las Indias" ["Natural and Moral History of the Indies"], in *Obras* (Madrid: Biblioteca de Autores Españoles, 1954), 2–247, at 161–62.

5 *Popol-Vuh*, ed. Adrián Recinos (Mexico: FCE, Biblioteca Americana, 1974), 99. English: *Popol-Vuh*, trans. Delia Goetz and Sylvanus Griswold Morley (Los Angeles: Plantin Press, 1954), 43.

6 See the essentially pedagogical topic of the "renewal of the world" in Mircea Eliade, *Aspects du mythe* (Paris: Gallimard, 1963), 56; and also, by the same author, *Mythes, rêves et mystères* (Paris: Gallimard, 1957), 254; and *Le mythe de l'éternel retour* (Paris: Gallimard, 1949), 83.

the chores that we recommend."[7] These chores are the community's customs and industries, the *ethos* of a nation.[8] The child is educated in the culture, the symbolic totality of a community, to control his instincts (as in the case of incest) and his nature. Fire thereby presents itself as the independence and lordship cultural being has over the world: "There was a tribe that stole fire among the smoke. And it was those in the house of Zotzil. The god of the Cakchiquel was called *Chamalcán,* and he had the form of a bat."[9]

Permit us a large and beautiful passage from the Inca Garcilaso de la Vega:

> The Inca Manco Cápac populated his communities while *teaching the inhabitants* to cultivate the land for their vassals and fashion houses and dig irrigation ditches and make the many things necessary for human life. He would *instruct* them in the civility, companionship, and fraternity which they should have with one another according to what reason and natural law teaches, persuading them with great efficacy that, to have perpetual peace between them and agreement, so as not to give rise to anger and passions, they should do unto others as they would have them do unto them, because it was not permitted to want a law for oneself and another for

---

7   Adrian Recinos, ed. & trans., *Memorial de Sololá. Anales de los Cakchiqueles: Título de los Señores de Tonicapán* [Memories of Sololá. Annals of the Cakchiqueles: Title of the Lords of Tonicapán] (México: Funda de Cultura Económica, 1950), 52.

8   It is in this sense which Hegel said that "pedagogics is the art that makes man ethical [*sittlich*]," G.W.F. Hegel, *Grundlinien der Philosophie des Rechts, Theorie-Werkausgabe* 7, eds. E. Moldenhauer and K. Michel (Frankfurt: Suhrkamp, 1969), 302. In other words, it follows the customs of a community, which gets at the "ontological" sense of pedagogics.

9   *Popol-Vuh,* trans. Goetz and Morley, 203. Following Freud and many other authors, Imre Hermann demonstrated very well in his *L'instinct filial* (Paris: Denoël, 1972) that the child, possessing the "grasping-of-the-mother" (see section 44 of the larger *Para una Ética de la Liberación Latinoamericana*) identifies the mother herself with the "tree," whose wood was used for firewood. Fire (which gives warmth like a mother to her child) is a substitute for the mother: culture.

everyone else [...]. He demanded the collection of livestock roaming the land without owners, whose wool he used to dress all in the community through the *industry and teaching* that the Queen Mama Ocllo Huaco had given to the indigenous women in spinning and weaving. *He taught them* to make footwear that even today they wear, called *usuta*. For every community or nation he formed he elected a *curaca* that is the same as cacique [...]. He demanded that the fruit of every community be guarded together, to make sure that everyone would have what they need.[10]

Every family, tribe or kingdom educated their children in these traditions, and thus:

I have not admired any other thing as much, nor found anything more praiseworthy, than the Mexicans' carefulness and

---

10 Inca Garcilaso de la Vega, *Comentarios Reales de los Incas* [*Commentaries on the Incas*] (Lima: Colección de Autores Peruanos, 1967), 5. The Inca Garcilaso is a beautiful example of the oral tradition's power in a community, for example, "this long account of the origin of their kings was given to me by that Inca, my mother's uncle, whom I asked for it, which I have attempted to translate faithfully from my own mother tongue, that of the Inca, into the foreign which is Castilian" (52). Culture, like the first and constitutive language of the child, is maternal: they suckle it. José de Acosta, in his "Historia Natural y Moral de las Indias," 196, tells us that "the Indians of Perú had also another marvel: from childhood, each would learn all the trades necessary for human life. For among them there would not be official positions, as there are among us, of tailors, shoemakers, and textile workers, but rather every individual and household must learn everything, and therefore provided for themselves. Everyone knew how to sew and make clothes; and this is why the Ynca, by providing them wool, considered them clothed. Everyone knew how to till the land and benefit it, without hiring outside workers. They all built their houses; and the women had the most knowledge of it all [...]. [A]nd in a manner of speaking, the Indians are similar to the institutes of the old monks referenced by the Lives of the Fathers. Truthfully, they are a people of little greed, nor are they lazy, and in this way they are content to live modestly, and it is certain that if one's lineage were continued thusly by choice and not custom or nature, we would say it was a life of great perfection." On Incan education see, among hundreds of works, Louis Baudin, *La vie quotidienne au temps des derniers incas* (Paris: Hachette, 1955), 94.

orderliness in raising their children, understanding well that all the full hope of a republic consists in childrearing and instruction of children and the young.[11]

Every family educated their children; not just kings, nobles, caciques or leaders, but the entire community. "My child, my gem, my rich quetzal plumage."[12] Thus didactic poems were frequent in American communities: "Lord, look at your longbow and sheath of arrows, it is my child's, oh Lord. When he is grown, he will give you a paper offering, oh Lord."[13] "You, my son, you must marry one who has a mother and father. Her mother, her father will not want to give their daughter to an excessively poor subject. You must push yourself to wake up early, to be active in the execution of your work."[14] The efficiency of pre-Hispanic education was proverbial, regarding compliance with sexual laws, speaking the truth and treating foreigners with respect.

Then the European conquest arrived, descending upon this world of Amerindian culture. The male conquistador became the oppressive father, the teacher–dominator, whom "commonly left no one alive in war save the boys and women," as

---

11 De Acosta, "Historia Natural y Moral de las Indias," 205. This is a chapter worthy of mentioning: "They sleep poorly and eat poorly, they were made to work since childhood so as not to become lazy people" (206). On Aztec education: De las Casas, *Apologética Historia*, 219. In chapter 122, De las Casas puts it this way: "You can see that the Mexicans were superior to many ancient communities in terms of their childrearing and education of the young" (297).

12 Garibay, *La Literatura de los Aztecas*, 107. There are beautiful recommendations for sons in these poems regarding lies and falsity, about life in the home, drinking alcohol, etc.

13 "Treinta y ocho textos lacandones" ["Thirty-eight Lacandon Texts"], in *La Literatura de los Mayas* [*Mayan Literature*], ed. Sodi M. Demetrio (Madrid: Joaquín Mortiz, 1976), 69.

14 "Un Señor da Consejos a su Hijo que Quiere Casarse" ["A Man Gives Advice to his Son Who Wants to Get Married"], in *La Literatura de Los Guaraníes* [*Guaraní Literature*], ed. León Cadogan (Madrid: Joaquín Mortiz, 1970), n.p. In *Apologética Historia*, De las Casas refers to a good number of these traditional maxims that fathers inculcated in their children (*Apologética Historia*, 300).

Bartolomé de las Casas wrote.[15] The Indian "women" became the raped mother, whose child is the Indian orphan or Latin American Mestizo. Before Mestizo children existed, the Amerindian orphans wandered America. They were the object of a pedagogy of dominance, as the conquistadors "came and extended their power over the motherless and fatherless children."[16] In any case, though not an orphan, the Amerindian child inaugurated a new pedagogical style: "Thus was born my son Diego. We found ourselves in *Bocó* (Chimaltenango) when he was born on day six of Tzi. Oh my son! We then started to pay taxes. We took so many pains to end the war. We were in great danger of dying twice."[17] Thus commenced the introjection of Amerindian *children* into the new colonial educational system and West Indian Christendom as a whole. Something was buried at that moment which would take centuries to recover:

> I found ridiculous the attempt to use masks of Bandiagara, African ibeyes, fetishes studded with nails, without knowing their meaning, as battering rams against the redoubts of the *Discourse on Method*. They were looking for barbarism in things that had never been barbarous when fulfilling their ritual function in the setting for which they were designed. By labeling such things "barbarous" the labelers [sic], though we can amend it, were putting themselves in the thinking, the Cartesian, position, the very opposite of the aim they were pursuing.[18]

If the Latin American erotic process originated in the conquistador's domination over the Indian woman, and if the po-

---

15 This is the epigraph at the beginning of the first published volume of my *Para una Ética de la Liberación Latinoamericana*, and is its frontispiece.
16 Barrera Vásquez, ed., *Libro de los Libros de Chilam Balan* [*The Book of Books of Chilam Balam*] (Mexico: FCE, Biblioteca Americana, 1948), 98.
17 Recinos, *Memoria de Sololá*, 162.
18 Carpentier, *Lost Steps*, 228. (This great writer's last book — *The Resource of Method*, published in 1974 — is a critique of modern Cartesian-European rationalism, much of which these short lines express.)

litical process originated through the Spanish murdering and dominating the erstwhile Indian, then pedagogical domination, properly speaking, began with the indoctrination that preceded and followed that conquest (and not by the evangelization independent of conquest which Bartolomé de las Casas, the Jesuits, or Franciscans proposed, with their abridgements and enlightened personalities from the sixteenth century).[19] In general, histories of pedagogy (as teaching and learning) do not emphasize how important the acculturation of Amerindian consciousness by the missionaries really was. The same may be said of histories of Latin American culture.[20] The Amerindian *world* trans-

---

19 See the difference between the dialectical domination which conquest supposes, and the analectic liberation quality of authentic evangelization in Enrique Dussel, *América Latina, Dependencia y Liberación* [*Latin America, Dependence and Liberation*] (Buenos Aires: Editorial Fernando García Cambeiro, 1973), especially in "Historia de la Fe Cristiana y Cambio Social en América Latina" ["History of the Christian Faith and Social Change in Latin America"], 193. Regarding the process of evangelization, see Enrique Dussel, ed., *Bartolomé de las Casas (1474-1974) e Historia de la Iglesia en América Latina II: Encuentro Latinoamericano de CEHILA en Chiapas* [*Bartolomé de las Casas (1474-1974) and the History of the Church in Latin America II: Latin American Encounter of CEHILA in Chiapas*] (Barcelona: Editorial Nova Terra, 1974), where you will find a short bibliography.

20 See my essay Enrique Dussel, "La Evangelización como Proceso de Aculturación" ["Evangelization as a Process of Acculturation"], in *América Latina y Conciencia Cristiana* [*Latin America and Christian Consciousness*] (Quito: Departamento de Pastoral CELAM, Collección IPLA, 1970), 74-76, at 74. For a sketch of the history of Latin American pedagogy, see Tomás Vasconi, "La Evolución de los Sistemas Educativos Latinoamericanos" ["Evolution of Latin American Systems of Education"], in *Educación y Cambio Social* [*Education and Social Change*] (Santiago: CESO, 1967), 39-54, at 39. On the educational problems during the time of Indian Christendom, see Felix Zubillaga and Antonio de Egaña, *Historia de la Iglesia en la América Española* [*History of the Church in Spanish America*] (Madrid: BAC, 1965), 597 and 1068. For a prototypical history of pedagogy, see in Esteban Fontana, "Semblanza Histórica del Colegio Nacional de Mendoza" ["Historical Sketch of the National School of Mendoza"], *Cuyo* 3 (1967): 43-88, and "Los Centros de Enseñanza de la Filosofía en la Argentina durante el Periodo Hispánico" ["The Teaching Centers of Philosophy in Argentina during the Spanish Period"], *Cuyo* 7 (1971): 83-146.

formed amid the ultimate foundations of Hispanic-European Christendom's culture and its preachings. In this Christianity

> the Indians, now orphans, the ties to their ancient cultures severed, both their gods and cities dead, find a place in the world [...]. It is often forgotten that to belong to the Catholic faith meant that one found a place in the cosmos. The flight of their gods and the death of their leaders had left the natives in a solitude so complete that it is difficult for a modern man to imagine it.[21]

This is how Latin American pedagogics began (Hispanic pedagogics as paternal and the Amerindian pedagogics as maternal): ideological domination in the name of the most sublime projects, delivered through the benedictions of papal bulls and of the Catholic Monarchs.

But the *child* in this case, properly speaking, is the Latin American Mestizo. This Mestizo, generation after generation, creates a new culture[22]; a culture separate, however, from every other culture; a culture that ignores its distinctness, that has not yet been dis-covered, where "[s]olitude and original become one and the same."[23] This new culture arrives "[o]f a nameless wrong: that of having been born"[24]; born of the Amerindian woman, born of

> the Mother, with swollen belly, which was at one and the same time breasts, womb, and sex, the first figure modeled by

---

21 Paz, *The Labyrinth of Solitude*, 102.
22 Gabriel García Márquez, in his *Cien Años de Soledad* (Buenos Aires: Sudamericana, 1972), 360, creates a hallucinatory milieu in the succession of generations in the small town of Macondo, "races condemned to one hundred years of solitude do not have a second opportunity on earth." English: Gabriel García Marquez, *One Hundred Years of Solitude*, trans. Gregory Rabassa (New York: Harper Perennial Modern Classics, 2006), 400.
23 Paz, *The Labyrinth of Solitude*, 206.
24 Ibid., 80.

man, when under his hands the possibility of the object came into being I had before me the Mother of the Infant Gods.[25]

The symbol of this violation is Doña Malinche, the mistress of Cortés. It is true that she gave herself voluntarily to the conquistador, but he forgot her as soon as she was no longer useful. Doña Marina becomes a figure representing the Indian women who were fascinated, violated or seduced by the Spaniards. And as a small boy, he will not forgive his mother if she abandons him to search for his father, the Mexican people have not forgiven La Malinche for her betrayal.[26]

The Mestizo, child of Latin American pedagogics, is like

a bleeding and humiliated Christ, a Christ who has been beaten by the soldiers and condemned by the judges, because they see in him a transfigured image of his own identity. And this brings to mind Cuauhtémoc, the young Aztec emperor who was dethroned, tortured and murdered by Cortés.[27]

Indian Christendom, with its catechisms, schools, and universities — from the high school in Santo Domingo in 1538, to the universities in Lima and Mexico in 1553 — created a Mestizo culture with a three-part internal contradiction. The culture simultaneously contained the imperial culture or "center," the high culture of the chiefly oligarchy, and the people's culture of the Mestizos, Negroes, Indians, Zambos, etc.[28] The people's culture,

---

25 Carpentier, *Lost Steps*, 165.
26 Paz, *The Labyrinth of Solitude*, 86.
27 Ibid., 83.
28 See Enrique Dussel, "Cultura Imperial, Cultura Ilustrada y Liberación de la Cultura Popular" ["Imperial Culture, High Culture, and Liberation of Popular Culture"], *Stromata* 30 (1974): 93–123, and an earlier piece I wrote before the explicit discovery of the doctrine of dependence: Enrique Dussel, "Cultura, Cultura Latinoamericana y Cultura Nacional" ["Culture, Latin American Culture, and National Culture"], *Cuyo* 4 (1968): 7–40.

the most authentic and distinct part of our new America, is consolidated around symbols such as

> the cult of the Virgin of Guadalupe [and many other invocations like that of Copacabana, etc]. In the first place, she is an Indian Virgin, in the second place, the scene of her appearance to the Indian Juan Diego was a hill that formerly contained a sanctuary dedicated to Tonantzin, "Our Mother," the Aztec goddess of fertility.[29]

These symbols predate the macho Hispanic conquistador. Thus "in contrast to Guadalupe, who is the Virgin Mother, the *Chingada* is the violated Mother."[30] The Virgin is the new culture, a mother without a father, unraped, pure. Here we find Latin America, the new, the positive, the mother without sin, undominated, hopeful; where the Indian (before his domination) and the Latin American are united in the time of their liberation.

Regarding that uniquely Latin American and mestizo culture, the people's culture, the colonizer's judgement will forever weigh heavily on it as the colonized:

> Who decides that laziness is constitutive of the essence of the colonized [...]. [But] the colonizer adds, so as not to give into the idea the colonized are perverse ignoramuses, with bad instincts, thieves and a little sadistic, legitimize their policing and just severity at the same time.[31]

---

29 Paz, *The Labyrinth of Solitude*, 84.
30 Ibid., 85.
31 Albert Memmi, *Retrato del Colonizado* [*Portrait of the Colonized*] (Buenos Aires: Ediciones de la Flor, 1969), 93. The similarity between Algeria and Tunisia in the twentieth century and the Amerindian in the sixteenth century is apparent here. One can read the judgmental comments about the Indians made by the conquistador and from the culture of bureaucratic, Hispanic, colonizers; in their seminars they said the Indians were "inclined to lust" which is why they could not be priests; "bestial and badly inclined" Fernandez de Oviedo called them; the American Councils (so just in other respects) considered them "rude" or like children, etcetera.

This judgment of the people's culture will penetrate profoundly into Latin America's new pedagogical era.

In effect, a new generation, born after the battles for neocolonial emancipation began in the nineteenth century, produced a rupture: "The Reform movement is the great rupture with the Mother,"[32] with the ancestral past, from Juarez until Sarmiento. "Catholicism was imposed by a minority of strangers after a military conquest; liberalism was imposed by a native minority, though its intellectual formation was French, after a civil war."[33] The neocolonial State, dependent on Anglos (meaning England and the United States), enacts a pedagogical betrayal of the past and dominates the community. In our Latin America:

> at the same time, one can see two civilizations on the same soil: a nascent one, which ignorant of what it carries on its shoulders copies the naive and popular efforts of the Middle Ages; another which without taking care what lies at its feet tries to bring about the crowning achievements of European civilization. The nineteenth and seventeenth centuries live together, one within the cities, the other in the country.[34]

---

32 Paz, *The Labyrinth of Solitude,* 88. This rupture with the "mother" is such that in the case of Sarmiento, it would be good to perform a concrete analysis of the mother–child relationship, to tease apart the sense of the negation of the popular Latin American culture as a *negation of the mother* and a correlating affirmation of the father (in this case, the successors of the conquistadors Cortés or Pizarro are England, France, and the United States).

33 Ibid., 127. In Mexico the emergence of liberalism is called The Reform Movement (c. 1857). For his part, Paz tells us that "the positivist disguise was not intended to deceive the people but to hide the moral nakedness of the regime from its own leaders and beneficiaries [...]. After a hundred years of struggle the people found themselves more alone than ever, with their religious life impoverished and their popular culture debased. We had lost our historical orientation" (132). Regarding the French influence in Latin America there is nothing better than reviving it from within the work of Alejo Carpentier, *El Siglo de las Luces* (Buenos Aires: Galerna, 1987), 29: "Esteban dreamed of Paris, with its art exhibitions, its intellectual cafés, its literary life." English: Alejo Carpentier, *Explosion in a Cathedral,* trans. John Sturrick (London: Minerva, 1991), 22.

34 Domingo Sarmiento, *Facundo* (Buenos Aires: Losada, 1967), 51. English: Domingo F. Sarmiento, *Facundo: Civilization and Barbarism, The First*

But beware! There are cities, yes, but there are other cities:

> [T]wo parties, one old-fashioned and one revolutionary, one conservative and the other progressive, both represented by a city — each civilized in its own way —, fed with ideas from different sources: Córdoba, from Spain, from the Councils, the commentators, the Digest; Buenos Aires, from Bentham, Rousseau, Montesquieu and the entirety of French literature.[35]

It is this moment of bourgeois pedagogical thinking in Latin America whose technical-bureaucratic ideal is the United States and whose cultural mecca is France.[36] The Project here is to in-

---

Complete English Translation, trans. Kathleen Ross (Berkeley: University of California Press, 2003), 70. Anibal Ponce, *Humanismo y Revolución* [*Humanism and Revolution*] (Mexico: Siglo Veintiuno, 1973), particularly the section on "Sarmiento y España," helps us discover Sarmiento's observational genius, and at the same time gives us an understanding of the bourgeois revolution's failure in 1520s Spain (a century before the English and two centuries before the French). It is evident that "liberalism" is nothing more than the emergence of a certain neocolonial dependent bourgeois in Latin America.

35 Sarmiento, *Facundo*, 59. Sarmiento explicitly proposes a "philosophy of culture." He calls European culture the following: consciousness, civilization, being, the urban; he calls the American the barbarous, material, nomadic, the countryside. One of them is industry, intelligence, beauty, reason; the other is uncultured, irrational, coarse, popular, Hispanic, medieval, Christian. "Quiroga" is taboo for Sarmiento, the Mestizo, the Latin American. Saúl Taborda importantly summarizes this in Saúl Taborda, *Investigaciones Pedagógicas* [*Pedagogical Investigations*] (Córdoba: Ateneo Filosófico, 1951), when he formulates the category of "the facúndico": "He who consciously belongs to a society developed in time in line with an incorruptible system of ends, will act in accordance to the profound sentiment of the coming of time and will situate himself in the historical direction of the 'facundican' state contained in the phenomenon that is Sarmiento" (Taborda, *Investigaciones Pedagógicas*, 230), which is rather "a conquest or colonization of one culture over another" because "Sarmiento's educational endeavor [has the deliberate intention] of submission to a foreign culture" (ibid.).

36 See Anibal Ponce, *Educación y Lucha de Clases* [*Education and Class Struggle*] (Buenos Aires: Matera, 1957), particularly the chapter "La Educación del Hombre Burgués" ["Education of Bourgeois Man"].

ject into the community a high culture (i.e., that of the dependent bourgeoisie, via obligation, free of charge, in the Sarmientian fashion via Argentinian law 1420) over and against the people's culture (i.e., that of Fierro the gaucho). This project consists in the community's introjecting a *high culture* that negates *the people's culture,* Fierro the gaucho's culture. This negation and introjection repeats the dialectic of conquest: a raped mother, a dominated father made servant to the new system, the creole mestizo, the son, the people's Latin America,

> They'll be wandering motherless
> like babes from the orphanage
> already left without a father
> that's how fate has abandoned them,
> with no one to protect them,
> nor even a dog to bark at them.
> Poor little creatures, maybe
> they've no place to shelter in,
> nor a roof to stand under,
> nor a corner to creep into,
> nor a shirt to put on them,
> nor a poncho to cover themselves.[37]

This orphan is acknowledged at "school" — an institution which Ivan Illich will call a *sacred cow*[38] — where he is instructed in a foreign culture, alienated from his people's tradition:

> And when they find they're chased away
> as you chase off a dog,
> Martin Fierro's sons will go
> with their tails between their legs,
> in search of kindred souls

---

[37] José Hernández, *Martín Fierro* (Buenos Aires: Losada, 1966), 53. English: José Hernández, *Martín Fierro: The Argentine Gaucho Epic,* trans. Henry Alfred Holmes (New York: Hispanic Institute in the United States, 1948), 31.

[38] Ivan Illich, *Libérer l'avenir* (Paris: Seuil, 1971), 120.

over to hide somewhere in the hills.[39]

In effect, hidden and living "mouth to mouth," the Latin American people's culture awaited its hour.

For all Latin America, the crisis of 1929 was a decisive moment for the awakening of a popular consciousness. The process of its occurrence anticipates this awakening in some countries (such as Irigoyenism in Argentina).

> The Mexican Revolution was an explosive and authentic revelation of our real nature [...]. Its lack of a set program gave it popular authenticity and originality [...]. The revolutionary movement was an instinctive explosion [...]. Zapata's traditionalism reveals that he had a profound awareness of our history. He was isolated both racially and regionally.[40]

The anti-liberal, national, and popular revolutions of the twentieth century newly affirm the mother, that Latin American culture which had been gestating for five centuries: a forgotten, negated people's culture. The revolutions negate the father through political and economic domination of Spain, England, and the United States. They negate the father through the neocolonial oligarchical State, but they affirm a new fatherhood: the liberated State of the future where authentic culture educates the child in its own home. *Rosario* would overcome *Mouche* (not just because she is French) for a time[41]; but the counter-revolu-

---

39 Hernández, *Martín Fierro*, 32.
40 Paz, *The Labyrinth of Solitude*, 135.
41 "The bond between Mouche and me was a habit of the senses, and not love... Three young artists had arrived... The musician was so white, the poet so Indian, the painter so black... The conversation had a single theme: Paris... [I asked] the young men about the history of their country, the first manifestations of its colonial literature, its folk traditions; and it was evident that my changing the subject was most distasteful to them... I saw them growing gaunt and pale — the Indian turning green, the Negro's smile gone, the white man perverted — more and more forgetful of the sun they had left behind... Years later, having fritted away their youth, they would return [to their countries], with vacant eyes... That night as I looked at them I could

tion of *Rosario* will quickly overcome *Mouche* in equal and opposite fashion. Ruth then prevails for a time, but not eternally,[42] because the *child* has begun an irreversible rebellion that will bring about either its annihilation or its liberation. "Noël vaguely understood[...] [that] bowed down by suffering and duties, beautiful in the midst of his misery, capable of loving in the face of afflictions and trials, man finds his greatness, his fullest measure, only in the Kingdom of This World."[43]

This rebellion of the *child* against the gerontocracies (the elders) and the bureaucracies — not that of the neocolonial bourgeoisie, but rather the society of opulence, the destruction and consumption of multinational companies — produces a new filicide and a new tragic pedagogical moment in Latin America. Now the youth, which burst forth in the University Reform of 1918, presents itself 50 years after the disturbances which culminated in the massacre at Tlatelolco (October 2, 1968 in Mexico) or in Ezeiza (June 20, 1973 in Buenos Aires).

> The Tlatelolco massacre reveals to us that a past we thought was buried is alive and erupts among us. Each time it presents itself in public, it presents itself masked and armed; we do not know who they are, except that they are destructive and seek vengence.[44]

Our new youth, our new culture, arrives here:

---

see the harm my uprooting from this environment, which had been mine until adolescence, had done to me... When the night enveloped me like a living presence, I found certain 'modern' themes unbearable" (Carpentier, *Lost Steps*, 64).

42 "Ruth, at the other end of the world, who had sent the Messengers that had dropped from the sky... and I had taken off into the clouds, to the stupefaction of the Neolithic men... During these last days I had felt the presence of Rosario close at hand. There were times at night when it seemed that I heard her quiet breathing" (ibid., 146).

43 Alejo Carpentier, *El Reino de Este Mundo* (Montevideo: Arca, 1969), 121. English: Alejo Carpentier, *The Kingdom of this World,* trans. Harriet de Onís (New York: Farrar, Straus and Giroux, 2006), 178.

44 Paz, *The Labyrinth of Solitude,* 40.

As people on the fringes, inhabitants of the suburbs of history, we Latin Americans are uninvited guests who have sneaked in through the West's back door, intruders who have arrived at the feast of modernity as the lights are about to be put out. We arrive late everywhere, we were born when it was already late in history, we have no post or, if we have one, we spit on its remains, our peoples lay down and slept for a century, and while asleep they were robbed and now they go about in rags, we have not been able to save even what the Spaniards left us when they departed, we have stabbed each other.[45]

The *gamín* of Bogotá is the symbol of the new culture:

The *gamín* is a street kid. He has no parents, or anyone to speak for him. He dresses in rags, he is dirty, he is hungry and sometimes begs for help. He robs and commits all kinds of crimes. He lives in gangs whom wealthy people fear.[46]

Gamín, the little orphan, the dominated child affected by a pedagogic of oppression: he is our subject.

---

45 Ibid., 228.
46 A. Villamil, C. Bejerano, and A. Cote, *El Gamín* [The Gamín] (Bogotá: Universidad Javeriana, 1973), 12. [Translator: to this citation was added "trabajo inedito," indicating the manuscript may have been unpublished. We could not find the version to which Dussel makes reference here.]

49

Limits of a Dialectical Interpretation of Pedagogics

The pedagogical ontology active in Latin America has as its wellspring a long European and North American history. In this case, to arrive at an understanding of our Latin American pedagogics' origin, we must include the culture of the "center" (like in the case of the erotic).[1] We will attempt to discover the foundation, the being of cultural domination's "mechanism" which, with few exceptions, is still practiced today in our continent.[2]

---

1   For a pedagogy of the "center" nothing is better than the historical account by Theodor Ballauf and Klaus Schaller, *Pädagogik: Eine Geschichte der Bildung und Erziehung*, 3 vols. (Freiburg/Munich: Karl Alber, 1969). See volume I: *Von der Antike bis zum Humanismus* and volume II: *Vom 16. Jhd. bis zum 19. Jhd.* In his 2,514 pages, Ballauf and Schaller not only give us an anthology, but a "European" interpretation.

2   For a minimal bibliography on Latin American pedagogy, beyond the works that we will cite at length in this chapter, see *La Revista de Ciencias de la Educación* (RCE) [*Educational Sciences Journal*] (based in Buenos Aires), which includes a good bibliography. See, e.g., Tomas Vasconi, "Contra la Escuela" ["Against the School"], *La Revista de Ciencias de la Educación* 9 (1973): 3–22. Additionally, see the book series *Educación Hoy: Perspectivas Latinoamericanas* [Education Today: Latin American Perspectives] (out of Bogotá), which has a collection of related topics from January 1971 onwards, including Jose Vasconcelos and Cecilio de Lora, *La Escuela Comunidad Educativa* [*The Educative School Community*] (Bogotá: Asociación de Publicaciones Educativas, 1972); Paulo Freire, *Concientización* [*Conscientization*]

Leaving aside the Greeks' notion of *paideia*, whose fundamental thesis we have indicated in another part of this work,[3]

(Bogotá: Asociación de Publicaciones Educativas, 1973); Pierre Furter and Ernani Fiori, *Educacion Liberadora* [*Liberatory Education*] (Bogotá: Asociación de Publicaciones Educativas, 1973). Regarding social change and education see Juan C. Agulla, *Educación, Sociedad, y Cambio Social* [*Education, Society, and Social Change*] (Buenos Aires: Kapelusz, 1973); Tomás Vasconi, *Educación y Cambio Social* [*Education and Social Change*] (Santiago: CESO, 1967), 117–30; Clarence Edward Beeby, *La Calidad de la Educación en los Países Nacientes* [*The Quality of Education in Emerging Countries*] (Mexico: Reverte Mexicana, 1967). Regarding more theoretical notions, see Alfredo Morales, *Hombre Nuevo: Nueva Educación: Educación en la Libertad y para la Libertad* [*New Man: New Education: Education in Liberty for Liberty*] (Columbia: Editorial de la Salle, 1972) and Aída Vazquez, "Problemas de Educación en el Tercer Mundo" ["Educational Problems in the Third World"], in the book edited with Fernand Oury, *Hacia una Pedagogía del Siglo XX* [*Towards a Pedagogy for the Twentieth Century*] (Buenos Aires: Siglo Veintiuno, 1968), 225–54. On history, see Luis Jorge Zanotti, *Etapas Historicas de las Politica Educativa* [*Historical Eras of Educational Politics*] (Buenos Aires: Editorial Universitaria de Buenos Aires, 1972). For more of a monograph, Juan C. Tedesco, *Educación y Sociedad en la Argentina (1800–1900)* [*Education and Society in Argentina (1800–1900)*] (Buenos Aires: Solar, 1986), as an example of a particular period in one particular Latin American country.

3   See Enrique Dussel, *Para una Ética de la Liberación Latinoamericana*, Book 1 (Mexico: Siglo Veintiuno, 1973), 130–40, in particular notes 354–58. This is all known quite well from Werner Jaeger's classic work *Paideia*. We must, however, propose further reflection. For Plato, and possibly Socrates, knowledge is "reminiscence" (anamnesis) (Plato's dialogues *Meno* 81a-82; *Phaedo* 72e–73a, *Phaedrus* 249b–c, *Republic* 476a, 507b), which is ultimately grasped through ontological dialectic. It is a looking back upon "the Same" (*to auto*) which we would see done among the gods (*Theaetetus* 191–95; *Philebus* 34). "[T]he Same" (see what has been said in Dussel, *Para una Ética de la Liberación Latinoamericana*, Book I, 104–6) is *divine*: ideas, yes, but at the same time this is *Greek culture itself*. Pedagogically, Socrates, through his maieutic method, brings to his disciples the *Greek* response to questions and thereby creates divine ideas; which is to say, he divinizes Greek culture. Subtle pedagogical domination! What is more, the pedagogue, who is not the parent of the child, takes on the parent's responsibility and occupies the position of the parent. As we will see, the disciple, as in the case of Rousseau's *Emile*, is like an orphanic entity before the despotic *schoolteacher's ego* which only assigns the orphan-child the role of *remembering* "the Same." All dominating pedagogics discipline memory, remembering: one must remember that which really has being is the master. How could I have forgot-

let us attend to the history of "modern" pedagogics. Basically, "modern" pedagogics came about in opposition to the medieval disciplines, Latin-Germanic Christendom in particular, in opposition to a new heteronomous authority, as Kant will call it, and concealing a new pro-ject which quickly appeared. To present the problematic, we must stop and examine the following ideas. *First,* as a fundamental thesis, in the manner which Freud wrote to his friend Fliess, it is necessary to comprehend that "our old world [was] governed by authority just as the new is governed by the dollar,"[4] and that the ancient pedagogics of the disciplines transitioned to the new pedagogics of liberty (thanks to the critiques of Vives, Montaigne, and Fénelon). Second, another aspect is the discovery that, in reality, the new conquering urban culture and imperial bourgeoisie culture negated and replaced feudal-rural authority (Rousseau's *Émile* is a good example). Manipulated subtly by the *schoolteacher's ego,* the disciple transforms into an *orphanic entity* (entity with neither father nor mother: orphan). This ego is the constituent which imposes the memory of "the Same" that the orphan is, and thereby prepares the disciple to become a member of imperial, bureaucratic, and bourgeois society. We will conclude with a third and last aspect, showing a contradiction produced in the colonies, where the enlightened elite remain culturally alienated and in blatant opposition to the people's culture. The people's culture does not accept the aforementioned pedagogical ontology of the enlightened elite, and so it therefore becomes impossible to accept theories like those of Pestalozzi, Dewey, or Montessori in Latin America. Let us summarize and look at all these aspects piece by piece.

"Modern" pedagogics (which would originally be called *the modern way*) has medieval authority as its foundational horizon.

---

ten, or for that matter remember, the *newness* that the disciple is, if he *has never been* but rather *will be?*

4 Sigmund Freud, *Briefe* (Frankfurt: Fischer Verlag, 1960), 244. English translation taken from: Sigmund Freud, *Origins of Psycho-Analysis: Letters to Wilhelm Fliess, Drafts and Notes: 1887–1902* (New York: Basic Books, 1954), 344.

"Modern" pedagogics rebels against this medieval organization of *discipline* in Latin-Germanic Christendom. Over the course of centuries "the Christian community organized in its bosom a bureaucratic-political structure (especially the Holy See, with its monarchic rights and ultra-center practices),"[5] which would put in place a highly productive and efficient educational system. The existence of pedagogical institutions (from Catholic schools to universities) is least important here, as well as the fact that the Pope assumed the ultimate position of *imago patris* (the figure of the "father" before the "mother" Church). What is fundamental is that the *censure* (in its political and psychological sense) is introjected by the guilty subjectivity.

> Here we have a new topic of research, thanks to which, according to my hypothesis, it is possible to establish correspondence between two existing planes: the *Superego* which tries to unmask analytical discourse, and the culture's *Superego* effectively exercised in a *canonical* text.[6]

The compulsory nature of censure makes it an inevitable imposition when confronted with feelings of holy fear. The potential penitent faces a lack which enshrouds him. He feels as though he deserves a tremendous punishment. The collective power of the parents and the State accrue in the sacerdotal figure, bringing it into being. This figure ascends to the primacy of "divine and natural laws" over "human laws," the "roman pontificate"

---

5   Pierre Legendre, *L'amour du censeur: Essai sur l'ordre dogmatique* (Paris: Seuil, 1974), 26. This suggestive work, which delimits the erotic in order to realize a social-political hermeneutic of medieval rights, lets us go from canonical text to psychoanalytic and political text. Do not confuse, in the following exposition, Christianity (a culture with which we will deal presently) and Christianism (a religion which will not occupy us here).

6   Ibid., 26. See in this text, particularly, the chapter called "L'ordre sexuel et sa terreur" ["The Sexual Order and its Terror"], 124–42 and "Politique des confesseurs" ["The Politics of the Confessors"], 143–64. This has nothing in common with the superficial and unilateral critiques of Latin American liberals. Consult also Gabriel le Bras, *Institutions ecclésiastiques de la chrétienté medievale* (Paris: Bloud & Gray, 1959).

over the "roman emperor" and "the clergy" over the "laymen." The sacerdotal figure produces a canonical pedagogical structure wherein the educated remains dumbfounded before the *auctoritas sacra*. We must remember that this canonical pedagogical structure has taken the form of a particular culture, frequently serving concrete groups, determinate communities, and certain historical interests. I am referring, in other words, to the equivocation on "Christianity" revealed by Kierkegaard.

Opposing the pontiff's ego, the feudal lords in rural areas act within the institutions of authority composing medieval censure. The obedient object of that censure desires something masochistic, and thus a new pedagogics arises to cast its predecessor as an enemy. This new educated subject's self-consciousness constitutes the ascending and expanding bourgeoisie. The city-dweller (*Burg* in ancient German) paves the way for a new *ego laboro*, building this new ego on the same foundations from which the first medieval hamlets arose in the eighteenth and nineteenth centuries. In opposition to feudal man and church, the *burghers* (city-dwellers) establish a new mode of production with the fruit of their labor. Their new mode of production has neither past records nor inheritances. Rabelais (1483–1553) expresses the newly-born bourgeoisie's aspirations in his *Gargantua and Pantagruel*. More clearly, Juan Luis Vives (1492/3–1540), in his famous work *De Disciplinis*,[7] criticizes the previous me-

---

[7] Juan Luis Vives, *Obras Completas*, ed. Lorenzo Riber (Madrid: Aguilar, 1947), 337–687; English: Juan Luis Vives, *On Education: A Translation of the De Tradendis Disciplinis*, trans. Foster Watson (Cambridge: University Press, 1913) [Translators' note: We follow Dussel's page references to the 1947 translation of Vives's Latin text edited by Lorenzo Riber.] Our critical pedagogue tells us in one passage that "there are such things that I would pay to unlearn as much as others pay to learn them" (Juan Luis Vives, *Against the Pseudodialecticians: A Humanist Attack on Medieval Logic*, trans. Rita Guerlac [Dordrecht: D. Reidel Publishing Company, 1979], 51). And speaking nonsensically about feudal education he says that "if the people understood such dementia, it were the laboring masses who would kick them out of the city, whistling, booing, rattling their instruments like they would idiotic people with no common sense" (ibid.). See Vives's existential distancing with respect to the feudal world and his closeness with bourgeois reality (when speaking positively of renaissance work).

dieval pedagogy as a "corruption of the arts, not as a fatality celebrated in this or that sector of erudition or culture, but that which was exacerbated in all people for perdition and ruin of the entire body."[8] The humanist bourgeoisie task

> for the progress of culture requires applying *critique* to the works of great authors, not just lazily relying on their authority [...]. *Nature* is not so exhausted nor so played out that it can no longer shed light on things as it did in the first centuries.[9]

For Vives, the horizon of his pedagogics is not disconnected to the idea, prevalent during his time, that "we venture to new seas, to new lands, to new stars never before seen [...] [and] it was with these prodigious discoveries that human lineage opened to the world."[10]

We can see then that the new pedagogics primarily says *no* to the previous culture (feudal-rural) without yet affirming the new man (imperial bourgeoisie). This negative moment is precisely the skepticism of Montaigne (1533–1592), for example.[11]10

---

8 Vives, *Obras Completas*, 399. In this piece, after a critique of the decadence of studies (either of the arts or the disciplines), comes a critique of each of the central branches of the fifteenth century curriculum: grammar, dialectics, rhetoric, philosophy, medicine, mathematics, civil rights and the very method of teaching itself. It is an essential work of modern pedagogy.

9 Ibid., 341. Observe the fundamental quality of the pedagogical problematic regarding "nature," that will quickly replace medieval culture. In Vives, what's more, one can already see the constitutive figure of the *schoolteacher's ego*: "because with it I — the preceptor — will not be harmed, nor will I harm my students" (ibid.).

10 Ibid., 338.

11 See the diverse interpretation of this thinker by Anibal Ponce, "La Educación del Hombre Burgués" ["Education of Bourgeois Man"], in *Educación y Lucha de Clases* [*Education and Class Struggle*] (Buenos Aires: Matera, 1957), 211. ("If chivalrous education no longer worked for the noble who needed to become a courtesan, then dialectic and theology worked neither for the noble bourgeois who chartered boats in the New World," 212), and by Max Horkheimer, "Montaigne und die Funktion der Skepsis," *Zeitschrift für Sozialforschung*, nos. 1–2 (1938): 1–54. See also Saúl Taborda, *Investigaciones Pedagógicas* [*Pedagogical Investigations*] (Córdoba: Ateneo filosófico,

Skepticism, however, has a double dimensionality: it can be the Pyrrhonian skepticism defined by Horkheimer (like a sickness of the intelligence), or a Christian Apologetic skepticism, like that against the Roman Empire. In this second sense, the skeptic negates the truth of an existing world while actively affirming a fundamentally new world (because every negation fundamentally includes an affirmation). Montaigne, as Anibal Ponce indicates, is skeptical of the feudal world given his affirmation of the bourgeois and imperial man. This shows not only a dominant skepticism, but also that which permits survival in tranquil irrationality, innocent and without risk. On the contrary, his skepticism (a century before Descartes) is a critique of the authoritative feudal pedagogics: the pedagogics of nobles and censures. To the children, he says:

> [L]et the diversity of opinions be propounded to, and laid before, him, he will himself choose, if he be able; if not, he will remain in doubt. For if he embrace the opinions of Xenophon and Plato, by the exercise of his reason they will no more be theirs, but become his own.[12]

Montaigne therefore shows a revolutionary skepticism peppered with bourgeois influence (since the bourgeoisie were downtrodden in the Middle Ages). He doubts what everyone takes as evident: decadent medieval culture. Today, moving forward in time, we Latin American philosophers are skeptical of the philosophy of the "center." We doubt its *universal* validity, but we will not proclaim, like the humanist and renaissance skeptics (who on their own formulated the bourgeois individualism as can be seen in the work of Burckhardt and Sombart),

---

1951), 113–47 (regarding the galant homme) and 161–64 (regarding the gentleman).

12 Michel de Montaigne, "De l'institution des enfants," in *Essais,* ed. M. Rat (Paris: Gariner, 1962), 156–88, at 161–62. For a bibliography, xlii–lxv. English translation from: Michel de Montaigne, "Of the Education of Children," in *The Works of Montaigne,* ed. W. Hazlitt, trans. Charles Cotton (London: John Templeman, 1842), 59–76, at 62.

that our horizon of comprehension is *nature:* ours is a *historical* pro-ject of liberation.

We cannot present all of the great modern pedagogues,[13] but we must not stop ourselves from engaging with the greatest influence in Europe, Jean-Jacques Rousseau (1712–1778). Of course we must focus on his masterpiece, *Emile, or On Education,* published in Paris in 1762.[14] To begin, we articulate our initial suspicion in terms of a pedagogical hermeneutic, operating simultaneously on the erotic-political level: the aforementioned modern pedagogues, confronting feudal authoritarianism, propound the liberty of the educated, a liberty to critique, doubt, and choose. This postulate of liberty, concretely, is the right proclaimed by a man emerging: the *bourgeoisie*. To educate the *child–youth–community* in the new world one must negate the previous medieval tradition. This negation of the *mother–people's culture* is carried out by the bourgeois *father–State,* following an English pedagogical lineage.[15] The passage of the erotic to the political is continuous: the father–State dominates the woman–people's culture (as feudalism commences). In the co-

---

13 If you read, for example, François de Fénelon and Octave Gréard, *De éducation des filles* (Paris: Pierre Emery, 1719), you can see, among other things, a machismo present in every line (*"instruction des femmes sur leurs devoirs,"* chapters 11 and 12, 65–79); situated at the level of the bourgeoisie ("She has the science of making herself heard [...]. It is necessary to choose the servants," 70), and how education slowly liberates itself from clerical tutelage ("I think you — the mother — could educate better than any convent," 86); etcetera. [Translators' note: We do not have the edition or version of this text which Dussel cites here. We have done our best to find these passages in the 1719 version from Pierre Emery, though we have used Dussel's page references.]

14 We will use the 1964 F. Richard edition (with a bibliography on xli-l). [Translators' note: Dussel cites Jean-Jacques Rousseau, *Émile ou de l'éducation,* trans. F. Richard (Paris: Garnier, 1964). For the English, translators have used Jean-Jacques Rousseau, *Emile, or On Education,* trans. Alan Bloom (New York, Basic: 1979).]

15 One has to realize, for example, that John Locke (1632–1704), contemplating bourgeois revolution in Cromwell's England, puts forward the anthropology of the *tabula rasa:* the man born without presuppositions, without a past, without previous conditionings. What an admirable educational prospect! Locke's philosophical work on education appeared in 1693.

lonial world, the neocolonial State symbolizes the father, embodied in the Empire's salaried teacher. The mother envelops her child; thereby receiving compensation from the male who treats her as an object (people's culture suckles its children on its symbols and purports to preserve them from the bourgeois state and its pedagogy). But the father–State intervenes between the mother–people's culture and the child–youth–community. Here an oedipal situation emerges: the child hates the bureaucratic father–State. Overcoming oedipal pedagogics occurs through negation of the mother-people's culture and by acceptance and identification with the father–State. The child–community, negating its mother–people's culture, becomes an orphan (an orphanic *entity* as we have said) at the disposal of the father–State which masks itself behind the severe and friendly face of the *preceptor,* the *schoolteacher's ego.* The preceptor identifies his state phallocracy with "nature" itself. In other words, the bourgeois man who relates to the cosmos in an attitude of exploitability (this is *natural* for capital: the flow of wealth via exploitation) claims that the horizon of his world is universal, eternal nature. The Greeks elevated their culture to the divine — when Socrates pretends that the responses induced in him are *divine* ideas — meanwhile modernity asserts that its *bourgeois culture* is *natural* (a nature which serves them as benevolent opposition to the neurotic authority of feudal medieval culture). *Nature,* being, the fundamental ontology of this modern pedagogics, desires to educate a child–community starting from the *tabula rasa* (because if the child–community was conditioned in any way, there would be opposition to modern pedagogics' educative work, an opposition distorting its dominating praxis). Without obstacles in its way, without family to predetermine it, without its people's culture to inform it, with neither a negated mother nor an oppressive father, the child–community is an *orphan,* a "child of nobody," the *Emile* (like Octavio Paz's use of the symbolic). Overcoming that oedipal pedagogics through identification of the child–community with the father–State is the repression of the child–community. That repression is dominating pedagogics exerting itself upon the orphan. In this way the preceptor that replaces the father[16] accomplishes its function as an employee of the bureaucratic State, which then replaces the people's culture (feudal in Europe, but Latin American among us). Universal *nature* identifies itself with the prevailing bureaucratic ideology, murdering the child (*filicide* that is *plebicide:* a death of the people). We see all this in Rousseau.

Our philosopher is a genius, and as such expresses revolutionary ideas for a new pedagogics. Our task here cannot be, therefore, to limit ourselves by repeating *ad nauseum* the oft-extolled virtues of the book we comment upon. Rather, as Latin Americans, we will suggest what is never said from the "center." Basically, Rousseau refers to the fundamental ontology of his pedagogics, the horizon that justifies his entire discourse: pedagogic *being* or the *pedagogical com-prehension of being*. He enunciates this foundation at the beginning of the book: "Everything is good as it leaves the hands of the Author of things; everything degenerates in the hands of man."[17] *Nature* is being, proper being, original being. But what is human *nature* for Rousseau? In the first place, we can clearly see from his comments that

> this education comes to us from nature or from men or from things. The internal development of our faculties and our organs is the education of nature [...]. Now, of all these three different educations, the one coming from nature is in no way in our control.[18]

Furthermore, nature equally opposes what we might call primitive culture, because "it is necessary not to confuse the state of nature with the savage state, and, similarly, the state of nature with the civil state."[19] Savagery is only a first mode of civilized life, and if savagery is better for Rousseau than modern man, it

---

16 Alexander Mitscherlich is wrong therefore, in *Auf dem Weg zur vaterlosen Gesellschaft* (Munich: Piper, 1963), inasmuch as the father masks himself with ambiguous substitutes.
17 Rousseau, *Emile*, 37.
18 Ibid., 38.
19 Ibid., 514.

is not because it is "natural," but because it is closer to a pristine nature. The opposite, the enemy, what Rousseau fights against pedagogically, is the "civil state," culture: "Prejudices, authority, necessity, example, all the social institutions in which we find ourselves submerged."[20] For our author, then, culture or civilization is a prison. Why? Because, in its historical and concrete experience, European culture, which is medieval, feudal, noble, and Christian, made itself felt like a *corset*, as oppression and repression.[21]

Human *nature* for Rousseau is composed of "original dispositions that everything must be related [to]."[22] We are not referring only to habits, for habits can be both acquired or natural,[23] but to spontaneity: "Leave him alone at liberty. Watch him act without saying anything at him. Consider what he will do and how he will go about it [...]. He is alert, light, quick, and his movements have all the vivacity of his age."[24] This is why our thinker has boundless confidence, because: "Nature has, for strengthening the body and making it grow, means that ought never be opposed."[25] Furthermore: "In the natural order, since men are all equal, their common calling is man's estate [...]. Liv-

---

20 Ibid., 37. "Good social institutions are those that know how to denature man, to take his absolute existence away from him in order to give him a relative one and transport him into a common unity" (40). "Civil man is born, lives, and dies in slavery. At his birth he is sewed in swaddling clothes; at his death is nailed in a coffin; so long as he keeps his human shape he is enchained by our institutions" (42–43). "It is here, from the first steps, outside of nature" (50.)

21 [Translator: We were not able to verify which edition Dussel refers to here, but we think it is Sigmund Freud, *Das Unbehagen in der Kultur* (Vienna: Internationaler Psychoanalytischer Verlag, 1963), 18.] Freud does not accept that culture's value can be negated in general. In reality, Rousseau does not negate culture in general but rather, clouded by "feudal culture" or the prevailing ecclesiastics, he projected his critique on this culture, on all of culture. Understood thusly the Rousseauian critique gains a greater importance.

22 Rousseau, *Emile*, 39.

23 Ibid., 39.

24 Ibid., 161.

25 Ibid., 86.

ing is the job I want to teach him [...]. Our true study is that of the human condition."²⁶ On the contrary: "Dependence on men [...] engenders all the vices, and by it, master and slave are mutually corrupted."²⁷ For Rousseau, *natura* (that which is constituted biologically, originary impulses, the tension in becoming that which one is by birth: *natus*) achieves, surreptitiously, a sense which is nonetheless full of content. It is visible here and there, so to speak.

Reading the *Emile* obliquely we see, for example, that the children's lives in the countryside are preferable to the opposite, the spoiled and deformed child of the city.²⁸ At the same time, we should be critical of the softness and stupidity of palace life.²⁹ But, in the end, Rousseau is inclined towards the bourgeois-industrial life because

> that which brings him [the child] closest to the state of nature is manual labor. Of all conditions, the artisan's is the most independent of fortune and men. The artisan depends only on his work. He is free [...].³⁰

But, furthermore, life's liberty must follow a first law:

> So soon as Emile knows what life is, my first care will be to teach him to preserve it [...]. You trust in the present order of society without thinking that this order is subject to in-

---

26 Ibid., 41–42.
27 Ibid., 85.
28 "Among the city children none is more adroit than he" (ibid., 161). "I see big boys in your fields plow, hoe, drive a team, load a barrel of wine, and control a cart" (166). "The first and most respectable of all arts is agriculture" (188).
29 "If he has the misfortune of being raised in Paris [...] he is lost" (ibid., 202). "Do not expose his eyes at the outset to the pomp of courts, the splendor of palaces" (227). "I would not want to have a palace for a dwelling" (347).
30 Ibid., 195. "But in society, where he necessarily lives at the expense of others, he owes them the price of his keep in work. This is without exception. To work is therefore an indispensable duty of social man" (ibid.). Rousseau finds himself, however, between two worlds, since he cannot but recognize (the feudal taste) that "agriculture is man's first trade" (ibid.).

evitable revolutions, and it is impossible for you to foresee or prevent the one which may affect your children. The nobles become commoners, the rich become poor [...]. We are approaching a state of crisis and the age of revolutions, [...] nature does not make princes, rich men, or great lords.[31]

This man, prepared for *competition,* presuming an equal playing field, nonetheless demonstrates his preferences:

> My furnishings would be as simple as my tastes [...]. Gambling is not a rich man's entertainment [...]. I would be the same in my private life and in my social relations. I would want my fortune to provide ease everywhere and never to create a feeling of inequality.[32]

Bit by bit Rousseau goes about designing the *ethos bourgeois* as a totality, for which he educates *Emile,* which is why Emile's education is finished with a trip through Europe, the delight of European bourgeois expansion.[33]

At its core, in its foundation, as a horizon of pedagogic comprehension, nature is taken to be the bourgeois world, which may be seen in the fact that

> The poor man does not need to be educated. His station gives him a compulsory education. He could have no other. On the contrary, the education the rich man receives from his station is that which suits him least, from both his own point of view and that of society [...]. For the same reason I will not be distressed if Emile is of noble birth."[34]

---

[31] Ibid., 194.
[32] Ibid., 347–48.
[33] Ibid., 450. On the other hand, it is interesting to note that, for Rousseau, that which is *useful* has more value than that which is *honest,* and thus praises those travelers who know how to *utilize* their trips and not simply become entranced contemplatively in front of monuments.
[34] Ibid., 52.

Therefore, improving the education of the bourgeoisie stands in contrast to the traditional education of the feudal world: the world of the noble, monarch, and ecclesiastic. The reigning "culture" is negated, and "nature" is identified with the nascent bourgeoisie.

Thus, *"Emile est orphelin"*[35] because every relation with his mother–culture must be cut for the sake of his being educated by the father–State (the French Revolution, that bourgeois revolution which adopted Rousseau as its chosen philosopher). The question is clear, and social-psychoanalysis can help us with the hermeneutics of Rousseau's confession:

> It makes no difference whether he has his father and mother. Charged with their duties, I inherit all their rights. He ought to honor his parents, but he ought to obey only me. That is my first, or, rather, my sole condition.[36]

At this point, the erotic contract and the *contrat social,* or political contract, have been made into a *pedagogical contract*. The citizen has no rights within the State (Hobbes's Leviathan) since these rights have been renounced within the *general will*. This State educates children on its own terms, and therefore the family and people's culture will have no say in the matter, nor have an opportunity to intervene as teacher. The preceptor (the masked father–State mediated by the schoolteacher's bourgeois bureaucracy) "always" has the child–community in his power. In this way, the preceptor is a master occupying the place of the parents because "[n]ature provides for it ["a state of weakness"] by the attachment of fathers and mothers; but this attachment can have its excess, its defect, its abuses."[37] Thus the preceptor supplements their deficiencies. Thus is born the modern "pedagogical institution," the school of the first bourgeois state, which later becomes imperial and simultaneously neocolonial, negat-

---

35 Ibid.
36 Ibid., 52–53.
37 Ibid., 84.

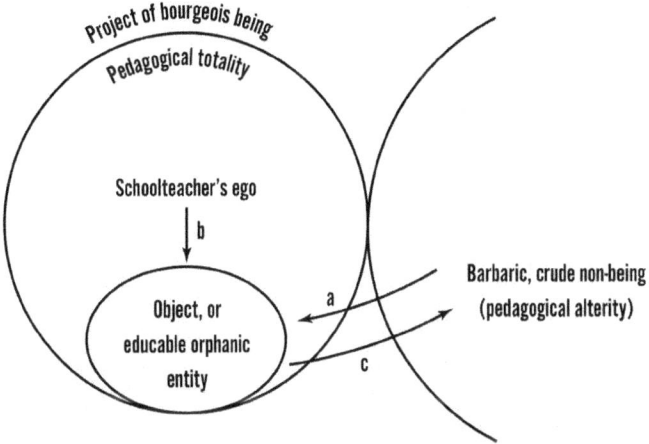

Figure 3. Ontological pedagogics of the schoolteacher's ego and orphanic entity.

ing its predecessor (feudal culture) and oppressing the people (the people's culture in the "periphery": our distinct and partly autochthonous culture).

Therefore, ideologically interpretive categories mask reality in a perfectly discernible way in Rousseauian ontological pedagogics. It is worthwhile to present a graphic which advances the material presented later in this chapter (Figure 3).

Rousseau consciously uses hermeneutic categories, telling us to "generalize our views and consider our pupil abstract man (*abstrait*)."[38] By the same abstract procedure, nature is bourgeois-European being, or the pedagogical horizon of bourgeois-European com-prehension. The preceptor is the constituting I and educator-as-such. *Emile*'s curriculum (that which can be followed step-by-step in the book's five main sections) is the order by which bourgeois man is educated through creativity, harshness, audaciousness, serenity, honor, etc.; in other words, those attitudes necessary in a world of harsh *competition*, which

---

38 Ibid., 42.

does not depend on hereditary nobility but rather the active agent's capacity. *Utility* is the absolute criterion:

> But will we make of Emile a knight errant, a redresser of wrongs, a paladin? Will he go and meddle in public affairs, play the wise man and defender of the laws with the nobles, with the magistrates, the courts? I know nothing about all that [...]. He will do all that he knows to be useful and good. He will do nothing more.[39]

Pedagogics are a moment of modernity's ontology. The constituting subject in this case is the father, the imperial State, the master or preceptor. This subjectivity understands being: he understands the project of European man, the bourgeois "center." The father–State–master is the *ego*, the positionality of support, the "from where" out of which unfurls the circle of the pedagogical world, and the ideological and gerontocratic domination of the child, youth, and community. The learner must obey the preceptor who has all the duties and rights of teaching (just as the State, in the *contrat social*, has all the duties and rights of governance). The learner, an orphan, whose memory of experiences is skillfully facilitated by the preceptor, is the *object* or teachable entity. The learner–orphan is educable, civilizable, europeanizable (if in a colony). We might say he is nearly domesticable. His subjectivity is objectivized. His other-world is ontified, used, manipulated, with the pretense of respecting his liberty. It is only necessary for him to be free of certain conditions (the father–mother, family, the people's culture, etc.). After he is free of these conditions he must be "led" (for this is *paidagogos*) by the pre-existing pro-ject of the educator.

These "categories" will be used by all the eminent pedagogues of Europe, Russia, and America. If we consider the work of Johann Pestalozzi (1746–1827), John Dewey (1859–1952), and Maria Montessori (1870–1952), to name three examples, we find the same ontological mechanism, a pro-ject of dominating peda-

---

[39] Ibid., 250.

gogy which they never name outright. The first of these tells us that "just as I see a tree growing, I see a man growing. From before his birth, the child has in him dispositions that will develop for the sole reason that he is alive."[40] This spontaneism, which we must know how to cultivate, will always hide the real intervention of the preceptor, who is an active agent introjecting the reigning pro-ject.[41] This is why Rousseau has such an appreciation for Robinson Crusoe, Daniel DeFoe's character: "The surest means of raising oneself above prejudices and ordering one's judgements about the true relations of things is to put oneself in the place of an isolated man [...] (*isolé*)."[42] In the same vein, in her well-known work *The Advanced Montessori Method, Vol. I: Spontaneous Activity in Education,* Maria Montessori writes that "it is the teacher who creates the mind of the child [...]. It is the teacher who has in his hands the development of the intelligence and culture of the children."[43] Maria Montessori's contribution consists of multiple discoveries in experimental psychology regarding the ways children better understand what is taught to them. This psychology negates, in fact, the importance of the possibility of Italian culture's teachings. But the teacher, as always, does not merely expand the child's natural dispositions, but rather ensures that the child introjects the proper dominating culture. We can see this in a reproduction of a dictation in one of the works of the aforementioned pedagogue:

---

40 Johann Heinrich Pestalozzi, "Semejanza entre el Crecimiento Orgánico y el Desarrollo Humano" ["Similarities between Organic Growth and Human Development"], in *Grandes Maestros de la Pedagogía Contemporánea* [*Great Masters of Contemporary Pedagogy*], ed. Francisco de Howre (Buenos Aires: Marcos Sastre, 1966), 280–92, at 270. See also Federico Delekat, *Pestalozzi: L'Uomo, il Filosofo, l'Educatore* (Venice: La Nuova Italia, 1928).

41 The problem of introjection (in Freudian terms: "Aggression is introjected [*introjiziert*], internalized [*verinnerlicht*][...]": Freud, *Das Unbehagen in der Kultur,* 250) is of the utmost importance in social psychoanalysis, since pedagogical institutions constitute the *reigning ethos* (which Freud would call the *Über-Ich* — ego ideal — or the internalized father in overcoming the oedipal complex).

42 Rousseau, *Emile,* 185.

43 Maria Montessori, *The Advanced Montessori Method, Vol. I: Spontaneous Activity in Education* (New York: Frederick A. Stokes Company, 1917), 25.

"Dictation. Italy is our beloved homeland. The king of Italy is Vittorio Emmanuel, and his august consort is the graceful Elena di Montenegro."[44] This is how the prevailing political pro-ject stains the *tabula rasa* of the orphanic entity (the child), mediated by the bureaucrat of instruction: the teacher!

But Emile will always be more fully dominated when proper political society and culture are identified with nature, with "democracy" and "liberty." This supposes an overcoming of limited individualism[45] and an explicit assumption of the bourgeoisie's social-industrial reality.[46] Thus pedagogy's function is to study "the way in which a social group brings up its immature members into its own social form."[47] For Dewey, the appropriate "social form" is that of his country, his culture: Anglo North America. *Being* is defined here as the pro-ject of the prevailing system, the child–youth–community will be educated in this system to "function" (here functionalism plays the role of pedagogics) within the reigning order, a fixed pedagogical totality. Bureaucratic institutions of education and mass communication will scientifically introject dominant ideology (following the best pedagogy). Imperial and high culture thus transforms itself into *repressor,* a subject Freud studied in *Civilization and its Discontents.*[48] Pedagogical institutions are those that permit "the culture to dominate the individual's aggressive inclination, debilitating it, disarming it and having it overlooked by

---

44 María Montessori, *Il Metodo della Pedagogia Scientifica, Applicato all'Educazione Infantile* (Rome: Ermanno Loescher, 1913), 230.

45 "Whenever we have in mind the discussion of a new movement in education, it is especially necessary to take the broader, or social, view" (John Dewey, *The School and Society* [Chicago: Phoenix Books, 1966], 7).

46 "The modification going on in the method and curriculum of education is as much a problem of the changed social situation, and as much an effort to meet the needs of the new society that is forming, as are changes in modes of industry and commerce" (ibid., 8).

47 John Dewey, *Democracy and Education: An Introduction to the Philosophy of Education* (New York: Macmillan, 1925), 12.

48 In addition to the work of Herbert Marcuse, *Eros and Civilization* (Boston: Beacon, 1955), it would be interesting to contrast the works of Gérard Mendel: *La revolte contre le père* (Paris: Payot, 1974), *Pour décoloniser l'enfant* (Paris: Payot, 1989), and *La crise de générations* (Paris: Payot, 1974).

an instance lodged in his interior, like a garrison in a conquered city."[49] It might even be tolerable to lament this if the cultural order was my own, was our own, a culture which everyone has procured together. It might be tolerable even if, as everyone knows, this "opulent society" is critiqued by those who suffer in the "center."[50] But the neocolonials of this "opulent society" must suffer the imperial cultural order, this alien and dominating pedagogics that is not our own. This cultural order oppresses doubly: by being a repressive culture as such, and through the oppression of national culture by another more powerful nation (economically, politically, and militarily speaking).

The *schoolteacher's ego* is an established dominator. We see an example of this in the conquistadors of America in 1492, who failed during the "crusades" in their plan to obtain "disciples" in the Middle East. This s*choolteacher's ego* must first of all take away the cultural dignity of the oppressed. Thus Gonzalo Fernández de Oviedo (1478–1557) tells us

> that these people from these Indies — though rational and of the same lineage as those from Noah's sacred arch — were *irrational and bestial* with their idolatry and sacrifices and infernal ceremonies [...],[51] and just as they have a hard head they also have a bestial and ill-inclined understanding.[52]

---

49 Freud, *Das Unbehagen in der Kultur,* 47 and 250. Reflect on the metaphor proposed there: "a conquered city [*eroberten*]" which expresses the phenomenon of "repression" (264).

50 Marcuse, *Eros and Civilization,* Chapter 4: "The Closing of the Universe of Discourse" (especially the section titled "The Language of Total Bureaucratization") and Herbert Marcuse, *One-Dimensional Man* (New York: Routledge, 2006) [Translator: We could not find the edition of Marcuse's *One-Dimensional Man* to which Dussel refers, so we include this 2006 edition for general interest);(Henry Jacoby, *The Bureaucritzation of the World* (Berkeley: University of California Press, 1973); and in Russian pedagogy, Anton Semionovich Makarenko, *The Road to Life: An Epic of Education,* 3 vols. (Honolulu: University Press of the Pacific, 2001) gets to the same point.

51 Gonzalo Fernández de Oviedo, *Historia General y Natural de las Indias* [*General and Natural History of the Indies*] (Mexico: FCE, 1950), 60.

52 Gonzalo Fernández de Oviedo, *Sumario de la Natural Historia de las Indias* [*Summary of the Natural History of the Indies*] (Mexico: FCE, 1950), 2.

Or the way in which Ginés de Sepúlveda characterized the Indians by saying that

> having cities and some rational way of being and some type of commerce — things natural necessity induces — only proves they are not bears or monkeys and are not completely lacking of reason.[53]

The barbarian is just burly, like a child in need of education, unto which the "gift" of European civilization must be given.

The saddest thing about this is that the dominating neocolonial culture has among its people many who would applaud the imperial mechanism's pedagogics. Domingo Faustino Sarmiento, in the nineteenth century no less, tells us that in Latin America

> at the same time two civilizations are seen on the same soil: a nascent one, that without any knowledge of what it carries on its shoulders is copying the naive and popular efforts of the Middle Ages; and another that without taking care of what lies at its feet tries to bring to fruition the last results of European civilization [...]. It is a struggle between European civilization and Indigenous barbarity, between intelligence and matter, a grand struggle in America.[54]

Sarmiento is part of an elite, an enlightened oligarchy, and it is to this oligarchy which Sartre refers when he writes that: "[t]

---

53 Ginés de Sepúlveda, *Democrates Alter,* ed. Alberto Losada (Madrid: CSICT, 1951), 15.
54 Sarmiento, *Facundo,* 51 and 39. See also my "Cultura Imperial, Cultura Ilustrada y Liberación de la Cultura Popular" ["Imperial Culture, High Culture, and Liberation of Popular Culture"], in the appendix of Dussel, *Para una Ética de la Liberación Latinoamericanas of Latin American Liberation, Book I*; also in Enrique Dussel, *Dependencia Cultural y Creación de la Cultura en America Latina* [*Cultural Subordination and the Creation of Latin American Culture*] (Buenos Aires: Bonum, 1974), 43.

he European elite undertook to manufacture a native elite [...]. These walking lies had nothing left to say to their brothers."[55]

Today, the imperial bourgeoisie's ontological pedagogics does not teach only in schools and universities, but also through subtle and ideological actions via mass media. Our children are students of Donald Duck, cowboy movies, and Superman and Batman comics. From these our new generations learn that the supreme value is measured in dollars, that being wicked means taking private property, that the way to re-establish an order "violated" by an "outlaw" is with the irrational violence of "the man." All this embodies the animated figure of "Patoruzú" (popular Argentinian caricature from an out-dated magazine), and alienation arrives in his paroxysm: When have you seen an Indian owning land in Patagonia? When have you seen an Indian living in Buenos Aires as a man of means? Patoruzú is nothing but a member of the landowning oligarchy disguised as a friendly Indian, who protects the "avivato" (the steward of ports' practical intelligence perverted or corrupted for the benefit of the empire) of "Isidoro." Everything in this story is insulting.[56]

The "orphan" *par excellence* of dominant pedagogics is not only the child, but the child of the periphery, the colonial orphan, the neocolonial orphan, the Latin American Mestizo who introjects the treat (imperial culture) by means of the trick (human nature).

It cannot surprise us then that the most critical student will be the university student, the youth studying in those underdeveloped and oppressed countries of the periphery. The youth thus transforms in a supremely lucid moment of the world-mechanism of dominating pedagogics. If a European author

---

55 Frantz Fanon, *The Wretched of the Earth* (New York: Vintage, 1963), 7.
56 Regarding our following topic, see Armand Mattelart, *La Comunicación Masiva en el Proceso de Liberación* [*Mass communication in the Process of Liberation*] (Buenos Aires: Siglo Veintiuno, 1973); Ariel Dorfman and Armand Mattelart, *How to Read Donald Duck: Imperialist Ideology in the Disney Comic* (New York: OR Books, 2018); and Armand Mattelart and Michele Mattelart, *Juventud Chilena: Rebeldía y Conformismo* [*Chilean Youth: Rebellion and Conformity*] (Santiago: Editorial Universitaria, 1970).

asks himself "why do adolescents focus on the tensions of industrial and technological revolution?"⁵⁷ then we have to ask ourselves: Why do adolescents in neocolonial countries focus not only on industrial and technological revolution, but equally on national liberation and the Latin American continent, or in Africa or Asia? The response is not difficult to proffer: the adolescent, youth (twenty-five to thirty years old, and younger), fails to overcome the second Oedipal crisis. In this second oedipus the father–State (or social authority) is not given as an "ego ideal" but rather as an adult in crisis, as a corrupted and corrupting State (whether it be imperial or neocolonial, he reads in the newspapers that the CIA uses eight million dollars to overthrow Latin American governments, that Ford intimidates the Arabs with the possibility of a war if they raise the price of oil, or that our governments do not have other means of achieving their ends beyond assassinating and torturing their opponents). The child of four or five years can admire his father (at least for his size and physical strength), and identifies with him as he "overcomes" the first oedipal complex. During adolescence and young adulthood, however, it is not possible for the young to identify in any way with him: they have no other option than to rebel against both their father and a society that does not give them much reassurance. On top of this, their professional futures are uncertain in the short term. This produces a proletarization of the university student, and thus the youth of the Third World have a privileged liberatory consciousness.⁵⁸ This consciousness is why students were assassinated at Tlatelolco Plaza, as you read at the beginning of this text in the epigraphs. The phenomenon of the new left is essentially pedagogical (and therefore erotic-political), and Latin America still has not grasped its originality, particularly the fact that it has little to do with apparently similar phenomena in the "center." Failure to

---

57 Mendel, *La crise de générations*, 137.
58 See Alejandro Nieto, *La Ideología Revolucionaria de los Estudiantes Europeos* [*The Revolutionary Ideology of European Students*] (Barcelona: Ariel, 1971), 267–77.

notice these differences, this optical failure, may yield lamentable and joint errors in diagnosing politics.

In the end we must point out that contemporary philosophy of language fully expresses a tautological pedagogics: it calls those groups in a dominated system "the Same" a priori. We will deal with this question in what follows.[59]

---

59 Albert Borgmann, *The Philosophy of Language: Historical Foundations and Contemporary Issues* (The Hague: Nijhoff, 1974). For an introduction to linguistics, see Gabriel Bes, "Lingüística," *Ciencia Nueva* 26 (1973): 8–14. For a linguistics of liberation it will be necessary to focus specifically on everything which is "put aside" to arrive at manageable "abstract objects" for science in order to take into account the prevailing "linguistic totality" and then be able to study "the oppressed" in this totality (or the excluded as "not-being" and thus "not-said"). Examining this we see that a language of "newness" emerges from the novelty of liberated experience.

50

Meta-physical Description of Pedagogics

Let us now begin overcoming the ontological pedagogics of domination. We will do so through a discovery of the child's exteriority in a pedagogics of liberation.[1] This pedagogics of liberation is an *anti-pedagogy* existing within the system. Against Hegel, we might define our *anti-pedagogy* as "the art of making unethical man (*unsittlich*)."[2]

---

1 For this section, beyond the indicated bibliography, see Paulo Freire, *The Pedagogy of the Oppressed,* trans. Donald Macedo (New York: Continuum, 2005); Paulo Freire, *La Educación como Práctica de la Libertad* [*Education as the Practice of Freedom*] (Buenos Aires: Siglo Veintiuno, 1970); Guillermo Gutierrez, *Ciencia, Cultura y Dependencia* [*Science, Culture, and Dependency*] (Buenos Aires: Guadalupe, 1973); Darcy Ribeiro, *La Universidad Latinoamericana* [*The Latin American University*] (Santiago: Editorial Universitaria, 1971); Hector Silva Michelena and Heinz Rudolf Sonntag, *Universidad, Dependencia y Revolución* [*University, Dependency, and Revolution*] (Mexico: Siglo Veintiuno, 1971); within a "developmentalist" vision, Jose Maria Echavarria, *Filosofía, Educación y Desarrollo* [*Philosophy, Education, and Development*] (Mexico: Siglo Veintiuno, 1967); from the United States, Noam Chomsky, *The Responsibility of Intellectuals* (New York: Students for a Democratic Society, 1966); Alberto Parisi, *The Problematic of Culture in Latin America,* 1974 [Translators' note: We were unable to find a citation for this book by Alberto Parisi].

2 G.W.F. Hegel, *Grundlinien der Philosophie des Rechts,* Theorie-Werkausgabe 7, eds. E. Moldenhauer and K. Michel (Frankfurt: Suhrkamp, 1969), 302, tells

Ontological pedagogics dominates because it considers the child–disciple an entity in which knowledge and attitudes must be deposited. These attitudes and knowledges compose "the Same," which the master or preceptor is. This domination (arrow *b* in Figure 3) includes the child in the Totality (arrow *a* in the same figure): it alienates him. In this case the child–disciple is that which is educable: the one who is educated is the fruit, an effect of educational *causality*. This causality is an ontic causality, which pro-duces something within something. The *pro*-duct (the "guided" *in opposition to* the view or reason which evaluates the result) is a formed, informed adult. This informed adult is constituted in accord with the fundamental pedagogical pro-ject: "the Same" that the father, teacher, system *already* is. Overcoming this ontology means opening oneself to an environment *beyond* the "being" instilled by the prevailing, reigning, pre-existing pedagogics. It expresses a meta-physic.

When they decide to give being unto the child, the pro-genitors, those who generate *someone* "afore," as we have seen in section 44 of the previous volume, open themselves to the historical future properly speaking. They open themselves to that which ad-vents the impossible, that which is not a possibility within myself nor our pro-ject. The "being" of the child is *reality* beyond ontological "being." The child is the Other: other than the pro-genitors; *always already* "other." The child cannot be a possibility to the pro-genitors because the child's being is not founded in their pro-ject, rather it transcends them. This is not mere transcendence, not even ontological transcendence; particularly for those children who overthrow this world, comprehending the horizon of the light of being, since the center of their parents' world is always "the Same." This transcendence is meta-physical transcendence properly speaking, because it goes

---

us that "pedagogy is the art of making ethical man." Of course he quickly warns us that "man dies by his habits, it is to say, when he has accustomed himself to everyday life, he degenerates spiritually and physically." Therefore, the *unsittlich* or unhabituated person we propose is not expressed merely in the sense of being active "within" the Totality, but rather is liberated "beyond" the system: un-installed.

beyond the parents in their being, in their power-being, beyond the most extreme possibility of their world. The child moves towards *an-other* world, towards the real constitution of *someone* "other." Regarding the child, the parents — because they are not mere parents of an animal or zoological individual (where the *species* is an insuperable totality) — are not the proper *cause,* nor the child a pro-duct or *effect* of their actions. This is a child, not an *entity.* The pro-genitors are pro-creators. With the notion of *pro-creation* we do not indicate a causal act, but rather a moment of *fecundity.* With the word "fecundity" we want to signal a human moment when one transcends meta-physically, constituting another world, constituting another human, or better: constituting the Other. It is a meta-physical act (and not ontic; it cannot properly be an ontological act) by which we want to indicate the abysmal separation of the instantiation of *someone dis-tinct* and not *something dif-ferent.* If *eros* is love between man and woman in the beauty of nudity, if *philia* is brotherly love found in the enthusiasm of the assembly, then *agapē* is the love of the Other that is *not-yet* real. Desire, which we have called "love-of-justice" (in section 16 of chapter III [of *Para una Ética*]) for the *nothing* that *is-not* yet, is excessive love *par excellence.* The man–woman face-to-face transcends in that *newness* where lovers see the face of the Other, the Other *par excellence:* the child that is not yet pro-created. The face-to-face of brother–brother, the face-to-face of citizen–citizen, each accepts the young, youth (not as a group of young people but rather what makes up the young as such: juvenility, as opposed to senility, for example). They recognize the disciple by giving space to him, treating him as that which comes from beyond prevailing being. Certainly the child-youth-disciple is never an *equal,* nor a different thing, nor an interlocutor "at par with the teacher." The child is *dis-tinct* in his origin, someone new, an eschatological history. He is messianic.

Paternity or *maternity,* as roles, may be cast as a kind of causality. In this case, the child must be the pro-duct of the thing close to his life, his career, his future: "the Same." *Filiality* would not be thus, but rather the relation that unites effect to cause, responding to what is pro-duced in him. *Filiality* responds to the expectations of pedagogical action, though this action looks more like domestication, ideological conditioning, and functional preparation within the system. *Filiality* is liberty, liberation, respect, novelty, and authentic history when paternity and maternity are fertility in gratuitous meta-physics; when they to want to have another someone, the Other, with whom to affirm, confirm, and transcend erotic love. Cause–effect is an ontic action with an ontological foundation; paternity–filiality is a transontological meta-physical moment which constructs a pedagogics' novelty. Ecstatic admiration before the face of the Other (of the erotic or political), understood as the presence of the absence of mystery, is the adult human's experience. Openness before the face of the *not-yet* of the desired child is respect before extreme alterity. The child that *already-is* is an historical continuity of their parents within the tradition and the risk of that tradition's alteration (and in this sense man and woman are more in alterity in their first encounter). Yet the child is also "afore" (if that word serves), since the parents love their beloved child that is *not-yet* with an *agapic love*. This is a love for human plenitude as such, where man simply desires to give *reality* to the Other; not to give a form to an entity (pro-duct, in-formation), but rather give a constitution of alterity to someone else. To pro-duce, even the most beautiful work of art, is to put a thing into the world. To pro-create is to let *another* world, a *new* world, be. It is to open from the pulse of supreme alterity the possibility of a witness which, from beyond being, is always the judge of the world.

Pedagogics is essentially the meta-physical bipolarity of the face-to-face of what is *anterior* to the Other, but in its beforeness what is always posterior. The child, pro-created by his parents (a *prius*) is that which reaches farther because he is younger. A diachrony therefore exists (a temporality which is neither coeval nor contemporary) that is very different from the synchrony of the erotic and political; one which makes both the erotic and political possible. The discontinuity of pedagogical temporality is essentially diachronic because it consists, justly, in transmission via transubstantiation — as Levinas says[3] — of human legacy onto new generations. But this transmission is not effectuated by generational differentiation of human identity. Rather it effectuates the legacy gathered in its likeness by a unique distinction, newness, the radicality of youth and student. The notion of *tradition* aspires to negate the notion of passive repetition, imitation, remembrance. Tradition is re-creation in a double sense: to create anew and to celebrate the appearance from nothing (the liberty of the child), the history constituted therein. This passing from exteriority to exteriority, from totality to alterity, discontinuously, as if by leaps, makes the human species an analogical species: a historical species, not merely ex-volitional and dialectical, but rather properly dis-volitional and analectical.

Paternity–maternity cannot therefore hide their anteriority, their tradition, their State–culture. The teacher is not an aseptic preceptor, identified with the gods or nature. The teacher is *such*, of a certain sex, a determined moment, a community and State, a nation, a social class, an era of humanity, with its doctrines and theories… He therefore does not have the right to present himself before the disciple as if he had all rights, and especially the right to be obeyed without limit, like the preceptor in *Emile*.

On the other hand, the child–disciple is not an orphan, though they have told him he is. Reigning pedagogics pretends to manipulate and domesticate him. But this is not true. *The other*

> does not exist: such is rational faith, the incurable belief of [dominating] human reason. Identity = reality, as if, in the end, everything must necessarily and absolutely be one and the same. (So says Antonio Machado, the great metaphysical poet.) But the other refuses to disappear; it subsists, it persists; it is the hard bone on which reason breaks its teeth. Abel Martín, with a poetic faith as human as rational faith,

---

3   Emmanuel Levinas, *Totalité et infini: Essai sur l'extériorité* (The Hague: Nijhoff, 1968), 294.

> believed in the other, in "the essential Heterogeneity of being," in what might be called the incurable otherness from which oneness must always suffer.[4]

The poet's formidable philosophical formulation helps us express our thinking: the child, the Other of pedagogics, *is there* anyway and against all pedagogics of domination. He is there against imperial and neocolonial forces, national oppressors or dominating classes, enlightened cultures and others. The Other, the child, does not acknowledge the certification which proclaims his death. The Other rebels, it will always rebel. There will always be reforms such as the Reforms of Córdoba in 1918, or Córdoban students, or the students in Tlatelolco in 1968. Wanting to eliminate the child-other is the same as pretending that he is an orphan. Without predecessors, they are assigned the system's deferred share: "the Same." In this way, the Latin American child is the victim of antonomasia: "he does not affirm himself as a mixture, but rather as an abstraction: he is a man. He becomes the son of Nothingness. His beginnings are in his own self."[5] But this impossibility is the fruit of imperial and national enlightened pedagogy. "Child of no one" is he who does not have his own culture, nor the people's culture. "Child of no one" is he who has negated the mother for the father, and negated the father for someone who playing the role of dominator (his Creole father has been similarly dominated). The *Emile* that can be educated by and for domination is a paradigmatic "child of no one." But, again, this is not the case. The American child's mother is an Indian, a Creole, a Latin American woman, or the people's culture, all of whom feeds the strongest resistance to empire at their breast. Furthermore, the orphan does in fact have a father: the assassinated or oppressed child, the Spanish man who forgot his spawn, the humiliated Creole. This is why

---

4   The first lines of Octavio Paz, *The Labyrinth of Solitude and Other Writings*, trans. Lysander Kemp, Yara Milos, and Rachel Phillips Belash (New York: Grove Press, 1985), 1.

5   Ibid., 87.

the child of no one is the child of the colonized, but the child of the half-colonized, because throughout his history he carries the memory of many half-liberations.

Neither the preceptor nor the child are autonomous or unconditioned. Both of them are moments in the Totality, *but both are at the same time meta-physical Exteriority.* This double analectic dialectic constitutes the anti-pedagogy mentioned at the outset: a pedagogics of liberation. This anti-pedagogy is a situation which is erotically anti-oedipal and politically post-imperial, both filial and of the people (and anti-filicidal and anti-plebicidal). The pedagogics of the face-to-face,[6] therefore, is respect for the Other, be it child or teacher. For the pro-genitor and teacher, the Other is the child–disciple: *the sacred* before which no love is sufficient, no hope excessive, no faith adequate. For the child–community the Other is the pro-genitor and teacher: *the before,* an epiphenomenal presence which exists as an original creator. This original creator is responsible for their being a reality. It is metaphysically impossible for the child to pay that debt. Parents grant being like a gift! The new cannot respond in kind with the same currency. His repayment can only be valid, in that moment, if he desires to return anew the superabundance in gratitude of new pro-creation. Yet this return must happen *dis-tinctly,* never as "the Same," always with a new history that impedes the ontological circle of eternal return. That circle imposes its iron domination, always articulating "the being is, the non-being is not." The *new child* is the factual demonstration of overcoming. He is the death of the Parmenidian or Hegelian ontologies. The *old* parent and teacher is the presence of existing history, a presence which denies us an existence like Robinson Crusoe's idolatrous "god" and its pantheistic preten-

---

[6] See the possible positions I have indicated in chapter VII, section 44, note 180 of *Para una Ética de la Liberación Latinoamericana.* Positions 3 through 10 are all properly pedagogical. The preponderant relations of pedagogical domination are the fourth (father–son) and seventh (father–daughter), which derive from the first (man–mother). Enrique Dussel, *Para uma Ética da Libertação Latino-americana III: Erótica e Pedagógica* (São Paulo: Edições Loyola-UNIMEP, 1982), 99.

sions to eternal dominance. Neither the preceptor nor the disciple are without condition. To be without condition is a false way of overcoming the Oedipus complex and political-pedagogical domination, since the father masks himself behind the aseptic teacher and the ideal pedagogics of the neocolonial and liberal State. In fact, the *imago patris* represses the child, *but without warning or notice.* The "center," the neocolonial State, mediated by imperial and supposedly enlightened cultures, identifies itself with universal culture, totalizing culture, human nature, *without permitting critical consciousness.* This totalization is the empire of ideology through collective communication.

On the other hand, the father, whose position is extended via the teacher and the State, does not have reason to interrupt the mother–child, the people's culture–community, if the mother has not totalized the child or the people's culture or community. But, as we have seen, the mother–people's culture tends to totalize itself within the child–community when, in the man–woman or State–people's culture dyads, it does not provide the required satisfaction. When the unsatisfied woman totalizes the child, the father then feels displaced. When the people's culture totalizes the community, the neocolonial and oligarchical State discovers its potential and actual enemy (the people's liberating nationalism). The father–State's repressive violence subjects the new (child–community), but at the same time produces a guilty moral consciousness. The child will desire its mother just as the community desires to live with its people's culture, which has been judged as barbaric, uncivilized, and illiterate. Repressing a love-for-justice with dominating pedagogics within the servile consciousness of the dominated (child–community) is an introjection of violence. A dominated exteriority is its result. If, in contrast, the father satisfies the mother in the man–woman dyad, she does not totalize the child. Yet this is a satisfaction which requires her to liberate herself (reaching in this face-to-face the plenitude of historical orgasm). In this case, the father interrupts the breast–mouth bipolarity (mother–child) as the Exteriority, as the Other, as the *poor* that interpellates the principle of totalization from beyond. He implores like a teacher, like a pro-phet who reveals future paths and calls upon the "vocation" of alterity. Exiting the womb, ending the weaning process, leaving the house to play, leaving the house for school and even work, some of these *exits* from the Totality through Alterity position the father as the child's "con-ductor": that is, his pedagogue (he-who-directs-the-child). In the same way, if the new, social, postindustrial and democratic state, the liberator, complies with the oppressed community's pro-ject, satisfying it with real social justice, the people's culture will not totalize the community as a State-sponsored set of oppositional, coercive, repressive, or leading institutions. On the contrary, the people's culture becomes the institution which serves the community as it grows from what it has received into what it is: its own distinct Latin American culture, which until now has been in part oppressed and, for the most part, a questionable exteriority.

The child, the Other, should be an *anti-Emile,* "Malinche's child," yes. It is not origin which discredits newness, but rather the way in which we assume that origin. Children of the Amerindian mother, clung to her flesh, fed from her breast, we enter history into the continuous discontinuity of tradition. We are not orphans. Let us simply recognize our real and humble origins! Let us love our mother. Let us recognize our despotic and phallocratic father. Or better yet, our despotic and phallocratic grandmother and grandfather. Our parents have rather been the community of colonial Christianity, the Creole whose father was the neocolonial oligarchy. Margarita transformed into *Margot*. We are dark children from the margins of history. Accepting our origin, we can be the teacher Latin American children need. This child, our child, child of those who have taken on trauma, oppression, children that have learned to forgive their mother and father, they will have a Latin American mother who will, for the first time, be able to nurse him on the smooth milk of her own culture's symbols. The father, a Mestizo, son of the conquistadores, son of the oligarchies and the rebellions and people's revolutions, is already the father–State that will not interrupt the child as it drinks from the maternal breast. On the contrary, he embraces both of them and brings them to their full realization in their authentic and alterative fulfillment.

Meta-physical pedagogics issues its question in agonizing hope, because:

> Someone is hearing me without knowing it,
> but those I sing of, those who know,
> go on being born and will overflow the world.[7]

Pedagogics essentially plays the part of Alterity in serving the Other as other, whether in the bipolarity of speech-hearing or questioning-listening. All this happens at a political and erotic level, because

> if the evolution of culture has such a transcendent analogy with that of the individual's evolution [...]. I would dare to maintain that the temptation to transfer psychoanalysis to the community would be something like a pathology of cultural communities [...].[8]

Or, perhaps, a cultural diagnosis of the individual pathology. Passage from the erotic-familial to the erotic-political is given by a doubly Oedipal situation: the *first oedipus* of childhood around four years of age, and the *second oedipus* from adolescence to youth (where the father is at the same time "my" father and the State).

The child is there. He might not have existed, perhaps simply because he is not desired, or because he is always avoided,[9]

---

[7] Pablo Neruda, "El Pueblo," in *Obras Escogidas* (Santiago: Andres Bello, 1972). English translation of "The People" by Alastair Reid may be found in Harold Bloom, *Poets and Poems* (New York: Infobase Publishing), 315–23, at 322.

[8] Sigmund Freud, *Das Unbehagen in der Kultur* (Vienna: Internationaler Psychoanalytischer Verlag, 1963), 269.

[9] See Carlos Trimbos, *Hombre y Mujer: La Relación de los Sexos en un Mundo Cambiado* [*Man and Wife: Relations between the Sexes in a Changing World*] (Buenos Aires: Lohlé, 1968), 155–250 , regarding the question of "conjugal relations and the regulation of births."

or because he is killed in an abortion. But leaving aside these *no-to-the-pedagogical-Other* (physical filicides), the pedagogical perversity par excellence, consider the relation:

(Father–teacher) → (child–disciple, the Other).

The child is born crying: it is his first communication, his first word, and though it is without sense it is still gestural and propaedeutically significant. We have called "moral conscience"[10] the knowledge of how to listen to the voice of the Other. There is no word so indigent, with a poverty so poor, so stricken with destitution, lacking in every security, integrity, protection, nourishment, and hospitality, as a newborn child's. Thus the child's positionality is two-directional:

> [I]n fear the child steps away from the object of his terror; he turns to the strongest [...]. Looks for defense, help, and protection beside the adult who is his biologically, in other words, next to his mother. Such is the behavior of small primates.[11]

After it has been born in exteriority, there exists a specific crypto-philic instinct (a love which hides and protects itself, like when a child covers her face with the sheets to feel safe in her bed), a totalizing movement and yearning to return to the safety of the womb. This is why the instinct to "cling-to-the-mother" is the first and most pressing. One must find warmth, security, protection, and nourishment. Grasping the mother's hands, feet, and mouth (or the primitive fur of the mother and her full breasts), the child can open itself to reality with confidence.

But at the same time there is an instinct to search, out of curiosity, separation, migration, and autonomy. This instinct is a movement toward alterity directed towards the constitution

---

10 See my Enrique Dussel, *Para una Ética de la Liberación Latinoamericana, Book II* (Buenos Aires: Siglo Veintiuno, 1973), 52–88.

11 Imre Hermann, *L'instinct filial* (Paris: Denoël, 1972), 155.

of an authentic world: first experiences, games, playing hide and seek. In this moment the father, as one who is not sexually linked to the child, plays his heterogeneous pedagogical role: he is the Other of the child–mother, the teacher of erotic and political exteriority. The teacher, then, must not inter-pose between the mother–child (and if he does "inter-pose" it is because the mother–child has totalized perversely, through the dissatisfaction of the wife-mother with the husband-father), but rather must advance himself as the questioning exteriority. In this position of liberty and free service (as that which wants nothing for itself), he can listen to the child's voice: "I am hungry!" Hunger for being, hunger for nourishment, hunger for culture, hunger for actuality. Listening to the voice of the child–student, the Other in its poverty, is the teacher's first imperative.

Pedagogics' Other, primarily the child–student, in its real positionality, either normal or an-oedipal, communicates what it needs in its exteriority, asking for what it is entitled to according to the rights assigned to it by the system, its biography, projects, hopes, and desires. To know how to listen to the student is to be able to be a teacher; it is to know how to take a humble posture before the *new*; it is to have the *theme* of authentically pedagogical discourse. The teacher will neither speak of, nor approach, the power of the pre-established gods, nor nature itself (which is of course the oppressive culture of the Rousseauian teacher) all of which precedes the student. The authentic teacher will first listen to the contrarian, provocative, questioning, and even insolent voice of one who wants to be Other. Only teachers that listen patiently, on the faith of his word, in a love-for-justice, are the hope for the liberation of the other as liberated. Only listeners like that can be teachers.

The teacher, from the Incan *amautas* to the Aztec *tlamatines* of Latin America, bends down with sacred veneration before the new and the weak. That is why ancient sages were also observers of nature, artists, scientists, doctors and architects, lawyers and prosecutors of those unjustly treated. Priests and sages served many professional functions in the first Neolithic cities. Contrary to our current understanding, pedagogics is not limited to the teacher–disciple relation. The doctor–patient relation, lawyer–client, engineer–population, psychiatrist/analyst–analysand, journalist–reader, artist–spectator, professional politician–supporter, priest–parish, philosopher–nonphilosopher, etc., etc., are all pedagogical relationships. The doctor, essentially, teaches convalescence. We will see that medical domination assumes a total knowledge of health and "exploits" the sick in their sickness. In reality, the doctor should teach the sick (and more importantly, the healthy) how to avoid their maladies and how to cure them using the patient's active participation. The authentic "professional" (in a noble sense and not its "structural function") enacts a "profession" of *service* to those in need of his "knowledge." Every profession is knowledge of how to "con-duct" someone towards something (from sickness to health — the doctor, from homelessness to a home — the architect, from everyday opinion to meta-physical knowledge — the philosopher, from youth to the state of adulthood — the father, teacher, from "abnormality" to "normality" — the psychoanalyst). Professionals guide others from a state of poverty to one of autonomy, fulfillment, and alterity. In this way the father conducts his son to become an equal, a member of the community, the adult Other.

The meaning of pedagogics, *a priori,* is to "listen to the voice of the student," his *new* history, his *revelation,* that which each generation gives without possible repetition because it is unique. The liberating father, not the Oedipal father, lets the child be born normally (leaving the womb), cuts the umbilical cord (first autonomy), lets him overcome weaning, lets him leave the house to play and go to school; not for the sake of the fatherhood-motherhood pro-ject but rather for the filial, meta-physical pro-ject which reveals itself in the *silence of the teacher.*

In adolescence, when primitive societies incorporated the young into the world and adult institutions by "initiation rites," there is a "resurrection of the Oedipal conflict"[12] because the de-

---

12 Gérard Mendel, *La crise de générations* (Paris: Pavot, 1974), 138. "In the present-day we confirm that the young person rejects identifying himself

finitive emergence of sexuality (as drive) cleaves identification with the father. Repression of one's love for the mother manifests itself explicitly in this case. But now, within societies facing industrial and bureaucratic crises, the young can take neither the "father-family" nor the "social-authority" as their ideal because both manifest themselves as insecurity, corruption, and immorality (particularly in the neocolonial State). "Youth rebellion," the presence of a truly emergent social class, newness itself ("young people"), is a phenomenon which belongs to the opulent society and the situation of neocolonial oppression. Young people, without "initiation rites" to reject, resist identifying with the father and the bureaucratic State. They resist identifying with the "system." Further, among young people, those who are more self-conscious about these situations are those that study. This is why it is not strange that social critique grows its most positive fruit through student actions, especially at universities, where identification with the *imago patris* is practically impossible.[13] Confronting this, the oedipal father (filicidal dominator of the mother) can adopt totalizing and alienating pedagogical attitudes. Let the situation "spoil," he says. Tempt the young people into becoming "fanatics." Terrorize them with murders and torture. Suppress the most conscious in general (students in particular). All these types of social filicide resist the same father (especially the neocolonial father), because this filicidal father eliminates novelty, critique, and the possibility of liberation. The student that does not want to identify with his father is an "anarchist" (who is not capable of judging the people's liberatory values), or is "archaic" (like the hippies), or is simply a "fascist"

---

with the model proposed by his father, by the adults and society. He does not want to be like them. He rejects the inheritance or what is left of it. It is something very different from a generational conflict, we propose to call it a generational crisis" (148).

13 See Alejandro Nieto, *La Ideología Revolucionaria de los Estudiantes Europeos* [*The Revolutionary Ideology of European Students*] (Barcelona: Ariel, 1971), 267–77. He concludes by saying: "In any case the powers that be will try to bury them with weapons of repression and the instruments of recuperation. Let us also state as a given that (youth) revolution will never be extinguished as long as the provoking causes are not eliminated" (266).

(in which case he identifies himself with his father-dominator, or even searches for a father-dominator in the State since that same State is in crisis, feeble, or mired in contradictions). In any case, all of these are pedagogics of filicide, modes of ontological oppression. In each case, the child cannot express himself.

By contrast, the teacher that listens to the voice of the young person, the State that educates its young people and community, must know how to stay silent at times, must leave young people to perform their historical responsibility. Adults are always ready to think that everything is at risk: the truth is that only Everything as "repressive system" is wagered. The repressive system is at risk because it dominated the community (the mother) and thereby interposed itself (between community and youth) to quell the young person's love for a free community. In the first oedipus the father's punishment was enough to repress the young person's love for their mother. In the second oedipus repression by the police and even the military becomes necessary: the young man is not slapped on the wrist like a little boy, he is murdered in Ezeiza, tortured, kidnapped. This is the neocolonial State's new kind of filicide. The father kills the son because he has already repressed the mother (the people's culture). The teacher, on the other hand, must listen to the voices of young people, "let them be," give them time, push them towards constructive action. The teacher must let them love, work intensely, and exhaust the generous superabundance of their energy in the service to the poor. This is what the young student wants, but the teacher-dominator will not provide.

Inverting the positions, the teacher appears as the Other. The student is in the Totality, the child, the young person, who is not an orphan but rather has a mother and a people's culture, a father and a State. Now it is the student who must listen to the teacher. The teacher, guided by the student's revelation, was able to "leave" the ancient system in which he found himself (which is an *analectic* existential moment of praxis with respect to the teacher's learning).[14] He committed himself to a practice that can situate him in the Exteriority of being, outside of "the system" because of his praxis in attending to the urgent questions of student revelation. "From beyond," now indeed, the teacher is the student's Other, and thus the teacher can "speak pro-phetically" to announce to their students the critical path that will lead them through actuality to their authentic future. The father–State is an authentic teacher when, like the Other of the mother–son, like the people's culture–youth–community, he proposes *newness,* that which is missing. He is like a fertilizer, like the pro-creator of a new process, like a critic which gives continuity to what the child already is. What the meta-physical teacher and the liberating State add to their child–community is the *critical* sense of *that which already is.* The child, young people, the community lack the discernment of that which they *already have,* between what they have introjected from the system (through alienation) and what are in reality (if they did not lack, then pedagogics would not be necessary: everyone would be adults and upstanding citizens from the beginning and there would not be history). Discerning between *the worst* that the student–community "has" (which, via introjection, negates the new because it affirms only "the Same") and *the best* that "is" (but which must be better in its becoming-being) is what the true teacher, the pro-phet, delivers as if it were a gift from Exteriority. Discerning between what the oppressor has constituted in the colonized, as his mask, and the beautiful face of colonized-as-autochthonic-other, the teacher's work is to uncover this distance. The teacher's work is to create the conditions for Alterity to self-evaluate. This teacher does not draw up the "pedagogical contract" that the preceptor proposes in *Emile* (which must be obeyed in full). This teacher deals with the already-existing student as such, treating the mother and the people's culture in

---

14 In Figure 24 of section 49 of *Para una Ética de la Liberación Latinoamericana,* we have indicated this trans-ontological action with arrow c. See Dussel, *Para una Ética de la Liberación Latinoamericana, Book III,* 178 (see also section 36, Dussel, *Para una Ética de la Liberación Latinoamericana, Book II,* 171–73).

the same way, treating the child, young people, from the community according to what it already is, according to what the community loves, according to what would be forgotten among so many repressions but was always already itself, like an Other. What the student is already is not some neutral nature (the *nature* of Rousseau which masks bourgeois imperial culture), but rather a new history: the dis-tinct child, with sacred demands that are unique and concrete. The orphan makes "universal" and "human" demands (which, to the reigning culture, are always *de facto*). The child makes real demands, historical and individual and non-transferable demands (which always come from the people's repressed culture, from the negated maternal relations, the authentic modes of an original and anointed time).

Politically, Latin American pedagogics begins by welcoming the revelation of the "Latin American being," *our voice*. Philosophy also begins here if it is truly the "analectic pedagogics of historical liberation." It is Latin American being,[15] national being,[16] cultural being, the project and being of marginalized groups, youth, Latin American children (such as the *gamín* from Bogotá)... The *symbolic* at the beginning of the last four chapters of this *Ethics* express the will to let our Latin America speak with a voice that in truth has been silenced, a voice hoarse from suffering but full of hopes...

---

15 See my "¿El Ser de Latinoamérica Tiene Pasado y Futuro?" ["Does Latin American Being Have a Future or a Past?"], in Dussel, *América Latina, Dependencia y Liberación* [*Latin America, Dependency, and Liberation*] (Buenos Aires: Editorial Fernando García Cambeiro, 1973), 24–36. (See also 18–66, where I pose a similar question.)

16 See for example Paz, *The Labyrinth of Solitude and Other Writings*, or Juan José Hernández Arregui, *¿Qué es el Ser Nacional?* [*What is National Being?*] (Buenos Aires: Plus Ultra, 1973), or, by the same author, *La Formación de la Conciencia Nacional* [*The Formation of National Consciousness*] (Buenos Aires: Hachea, 1960). This theme is becoming increasingly important and the question "national being" is taking root in all Latin American countries. Sometimes derived as mere indigeneity, or in the negritud of the *bantú* (for those nations which are predominantly black), or in *"literatura."* In any case, the "necessity" of self-definition indicates a pedagogical reality: the child-student-community desires to speak its piece, desires to say *who it is*.

The child–community, the pedagogics' poor, is not an *orphanic entity* kneeling before a *schoolteacher's ego* like the reigning pedagogy teaches us. The child–community is *original* Exteriority: the fountain of the future, re-novation, life that is dis-tinct, a political and familial ad-venture. It is an original Alterity of the new world.

51

Economy and Pedagogics

The "economic" of the face-to-face pedagogic is quite unique and particular. It is distinct from the "economic" vis-à-vis the erotic or the political. Erotic and political *proximity* demands, for its permanence, the *distance* of economic work. On the other hand, *proximity* in pedagogics is always already "economic" because *distance,* at the onset, is the child's pre-play (in the newborn's first experiences of hearing, seeing, smelling, moving her hands, etc.). Shortly after this *distance* comes a pre-work: play, humanity's first non-pragmatic relationship with nature. Pre-work is merely preparation for the pragmatism of the erotic or political "economy." *Proximity,* the child–mother face-to-face at the breast, the children–parents face-to-face at the family table, or at a banquet or party or a political celebration, is at the same time a "face-to-face." *Proximity* is immediacy. The classroom, a teacher's exposition, is also a face-to-face and therefore a form of nourishment. This is why in the "pedagogical economy," which begins with someone providing nourishment with their breast, ends with learning how to consume a final remedy in the face of the retired elder's impending death, living the post-pragmatic life. The adult secures through her work housing, clothing, food and political structure, which the child receives by nature of being progeny (thus the responsibility to be part of the next generation continues itself through pedagogics as an ongoing historical regeneration). The one who suckles never worked for this nourishment in the first place. In this case there is no deferment of pleasure for work, but rather a deferment of work for the pleasure of play. Let us consider this problematic more precisely.[1]

The most resounding argument for the meta-physics of alterity against ontology (or the economic relation between humans and nature, or between humans and birth as their origin in the world) is that the humans are born from humans and their first relation is with humans, not nature. We are born in *someone's* uterus. *Someone* feeds us. Put even more strongly: we eat someone. The son-mother relationship is the *veritas prima*, the original experience. On this point we do not agree with Rascovsky when he tells us that "intrauterine mammalian development begins with the oral-cannibalistic phase in which the infant is fed, by suction, from body parts of the mother [...]."[2] In reality,

---

1 Latin America has been more original on this topic than any other area of human knowledge. See Ivan Illich, *Une société sans école* (Paris: Seuil, 1971), and by the same author, *Libérer l'avenir* (Paris: Seuil, 1971) (both books are the result of work by Illich at the CIDOC in Cuernavaca, Mexico). [Available English translation: *Deschooling Society* (London: Marion Boyars, 1996)]; Ivan Illich, *Alternativas al Médico* (Cuernavaca: CIDOC, 1974); Ivan Illich, *Alternativas al Transporte* [*Alternatives to Transportation*] (Cuernavaca: CIDOC, 1974); Ivan Ilich, *Hacia una Sociedad Convivencial* (Cuernavaca: CIDOC, 1972) English: Ivan Illich, *Limits to Medicine: Medical Nemesis, the Expropriation of Health* (London: Marion Boyars, 2000) and Ivan Illich, *Tools for Conviviality* (London: Marion Boyars, 2001). This last piece requires previous knowledge of a report by MIT for the Rome Club, elaborated by Donella Meadows, Joergen Randers, and William Behrens, *The Limits of Growth* (New York: Universe Books, 1972). Furthermore, from among the immense bibliography on pedagogy and educative reality in Latin America, we want to indicate the "Decreto Ley 19326" ["Decree Law 19326"] or "Ley General de Educación" ["General Law of Education"] of Perú and "Reforma de la Educación Peruana: Informe General" ["Peruvian Educational Reform: General Report"] by the Reform Commission in Lima, 1970, in which the philosopher Augusto Salazar Bondy intervened actively, *Ley General de Educación del Perú* (Lima: Decreto Ley, 1972).

2 Arnaldo Rascovsky, *El Filicidio* [*Filicide*] (Buenos Aires: Orion, 1973), 23. The pre-human mammal is like a zoological preparation of human alterity.

the normal relationship among animals is not cannibalistic, and much less so humans, due to the specific instinct against destroying individuals of the same species. This is also the case because the mother, as the Other, is experienced as someone and not something. Cannibalism is perversity, a form of schizo-paranoia. The mother's ability to nourish is an alternative relation, which at the same time establishes a face-to-face relationship in the intimacy of its embrace, the child receiving nourishment as a gift. Cannibalism positions the mother as something, an object. To suckle is rather to receive "something" from *someone:* milk, food. The truth is that during the postpartum period (from birth to weaning) the child cannot distinguish between the pleasure of his guardian's embrace, the pleasure of labial suction, the contact of the mother's breast, and the flavorful lukewarm liquids which his taste buds sense. This is therefore very far from a reduction of the Other to a mere edible thing.

Newborn primates desperately seek the nourishing breast, and without help from their mothers.[3] With humans, however, the pedagogical task is immediate, as the child does not have an instinct to "cling-to-the-mother" (of course, they do not have fur to which they might cling). The mother must put the child's mouth on her nipple. The immediacy of the *mouth–nipple* relation is not like some totalizing cannibalistic action but more like a fulfilment of alterative mutual drive (the child seeking nourishing warmth, protection…; the mother giving nourishment-warmth-love…). This moment is the moment from which originates, like a primal fountain, all future relations: human–human and human–nature. We might say that history, culture, the erotic and the political (even archeology) are all born in the immediacy of that moment of "being-suckling"; some through dis-tinction, or alternatively through di-fference. The ecstasy of "being-suckling" is the archaic nucleus of Totality–Alterity. In

---

Oviparous animals, on the other hand, are born in an animal-nature relation and the pedagogical process is minimal, in some species pedagogy is null and all is purely specific instinct.

3   Imre Hermann, "El Instinto de Nutrición," in *L'instinct filial* (Paris: Denoël, 1972), 71–83.

this "being-suckling" moment there is no space or distance, but rather *proximity:* hand grasps breast (it does not work or play); a smooth and liberated mouth (like dogs or grazing animals) maintains a constantly nourishing kiss (which is neither a shout nor protest nor a declaration of erotic love nor a proclamation in the marketplace); the body lays in warmth (a warmth which has not yet risen like a flame); helpless feet rest (not yet suffering wounds from running endless paths). Humanity is still one and undifferentiated in this "being-suckling." Pedagogics will be, in an exact and precise way, knowledge of entering the *distance*. Teaching an abandonment of *proximity* satisfying the child like a gift given (not earned) will structure a *distance* which constructs an *earned proximity* (through work).

The primate mother cleans her child's skin (Hermann calls it "servicing the skin"[4]), and little by little she raises the child to be able to climb, swing, jump, walk, and run. The mother does all of this over and over again, with infinite patience. As part of the same process the primate mother steps back from the constant care of her children so they can learn to complete life's everyday tasks. Thus she builds up their autonomy.[5] In any case, the primate's pedagogics is very limited: a life lead by instinct quickly puts an end to their possibilities.

Anthropological pedagogics, on the other hand, has limitless possibilities. Instincts are guided towards humanity's erotic and political life through the process known as socialization. A life of the instincts (situated in the brain's diencephalon region) gives way to humanity's erotic-political life (which is situated in the neocortex): phylogenetic evolution (the life of a species) brings pedagogy to an ontogenetic level (in every human's life).[6] When the instincts adapt to alterity, this adaptation serves as the

---

4   Ibid., 295.
5   Ibid., 296–99.
6   The works of Piaget, for example, must be situated in this context: certainly limited by his experiences in "central-imperial" cultures, his conclusions are an important move forward in the study of the genetic structuration and the child's primal evolution. It would be necessary to modify his hypothesis to begin thinking about the pedagogical reality of the "periphery."

opening of the Other as other, and the overcoming of a primal totality. Education completes this dif-ferentiating function, distinguishing the many moments of the archaic *nucleus* of "being-suckling" into *mouth-hands-feet*.

At first through imitation, and then practically through domestication (what the French would call "dressage") the "hands" begin to *play* within the space perceivable by the eye. Primate hands have to grasp the mother's hair. A baby human's hands are free, every finger with a unique cortical region, to begin its history — which is still non-productive. Therefore, in play (the first *distance*) *homo faber* emerges, who, climbing down the tree, adopted an erect position and then lit a *fire* with that same tree (which signifies the *symbolic mother*). This is the beginning of industry.[7]

In the same way hands let go of the breast, the "mouth" differentiates its function from nourishment to communication and signification. The human mouth, which for millennia has not been part of the aggressive instinct (such as the orangutan's bite), articulates *language,* the mother tongue, the people's language. When, at approximately seven weeks old, the mother has a "diminution of lactation"[8] a fracture erupts in the mother–child relation, leaving "space" for the appearance of the father (who renews his relationship with the mother as well). This accelerates the alterative pedagogical process.

Third, the child begins to use his "feet," crawling at first and then walking. His *ludic space* widens, and with it his world. Thus begins a search and discovery of quotidian novelties which populate his growing experience's horizon. *Distance* develops. *Proximity,* that of "being-suckling," has been left behind for more open spaces and situations which, when they achieve their maximum distance (in fellow adults), will mean the child is prepared for the most intense proximity: erotic coitus between educated man and woman.

---

7   Hermann, *L'instinct filial,* 370.
8   Rascovsky, *El Filicidio,* 32.

By crawling, one can turn on the TV. Walking out of the front door gets one neck deep in possible paths (the world of transportation), the countryside, the neighborhood, the city. The contents of opulent society and undeveloped and oppressed communities find their way into the senses: objects into the hands, impressions into the eyes, noises into the ears. Growing up, one overcomes Oedipal identification with the father. The child thus arrives at "school," the pedagogical-political institution. From the house (with its erotic pedagogics) to school and the mass media (with their political pedagogics), customs (*ethos*), and institutions (State) form and imprison the child. In Latin America, and throughout the "periphery," the question of the "economic" and pedagogics must be situated at a political level, because the pressures of the imperial system and the arrested development it enforces turns education into the community's essential political task. Here we have a critique of prevailing *pedagogical institutions* in the dependent nations, maintained by the poor neocolonial States. It may appear that success in life is the purpose of the "pedagogical system." But

> achieving success in school, work, and love is a combination which only a minority of people in Latin America can reach, about 1–5% of people. The winners know that this is how to keep the rate of their income above the national average; they are also the only ones who have access to political power, which they will use as a powerful tool to promote their ancestry.[9]

Let us make another fundamental clarification. *Pedagogics* must not be reduced to the school–student relation, or to those institutions which we commonly associate with pedagogy. For us, throughout this entire chapter of *Ethics of Latin American Liberation,* pedagogics includes all institutional *services* (in its social, political, and economic sense), which are essentially of

---

9   Illich, *Limits to Medicine*, 1.

three types: education, health, and welfare.[10] The last includes housing, social security, transportation, etcetera.

The child's transition from a domestic-erotic pedagogics to a political pedagogics also means shifting from a focus on *play* to one of planned *learning,* which is to say study, and education within the institutions. This education is still not economic work. Erotic pedagogics articulates the relationship with the parents; whereas political pedagogics encompasses the relationship with the State, social classes, both the dominant and people's cultures, science, technology, mass communication, etc. The child's transition is therefore a movement from the psychic to the social[11]; a movement towards political space.

This is the point at which *economic* pedagogics acquires its fullest meaning. We now turn to the relationship between humans and nature, as a face-to-face of *distance,* which we will call pedagogical "systems": "educational system," "healthcare system," "welfare system," etc. These "systems" have unique histories, they respond to particular demands and interests, fulfill particular purposes, have concrete operating procedures, and entail specific and determined *costs* for societies. We are told that

> in Latin America, of those that enter primary schools (and in certain countries, this is only 20% of the population) less

---

10 Rick Carlson's excellent book, *The End of Medicine* (New York: John Wiley & Sons, 1975), cited in Illich's above-mentioned *Limits to Medicine,* clearly states on page 39 that "obviously by services I include all of them, from TWA to fast food restaurants. But it is estimated that the largest expansion in the future will take place in educational services, in health and welfare, which have been officially turned into bureaucracies."

11 This passage is contrary and has a different sense than the passage indicated by Gérard Mendel in "De la régression du politique au psychique," *Sociopsychanalyse* 1 (1972): 11–63, at 16, when he tells us "the regression of the political to the psychical happens when the social conflict cannot basically effect itself." Police repression drifts from the social conflict in introjected psychological conflict. On the other hand, when the child reaches five years of age, overcoming the oedipus complex, thus begins his propaedeutic entrance into the political (his real entrance will come during adolescence).

than 27% graduate to secondary school, and 1% get a university diploma. However, no government devotes less than 18% of the national budget for education and some devote even 30%. The fact is that the financial structures prohibit further promotion of schooling, as defined in industrial society. The annual cost per student in the United States — between the ages of twelve and twenty-four — is equal to the gross national product of many Latin Americans over a period of two to three years. School is extremely expensive for developing nations.[12]

What we suspect is the following: "systems" such as education, health, the courts (from the tribunals to the lawyers), and transportation, just to name a few, constitute self-sustaining Totalities which have begun to *exploit* those they purport to serve. We will argue that, in fact, the educational "system" alienates the student, the healthcare system makes the healthy sick, the courts create new obligations and hand down verdicts through huge expense (where justice does not matter at all), and transportation systems cause people to waste more time getting where they want to go than in the hamlets of colonial Christendom. These "systems" sustain themselves, regulate themselves, and impede the general good to such an extent that any foreign layperson can pass judgement on their usefulness (how could someone without a license chair a department of teacher education? How could someone without years of medical training evaluate medicinal training? How would someone who is not a lawyer dare to make a judgement in a penal case?). They assume the exclusive right to educate those entering political society through a sacred and highly sophisticated liturgy, and they maintain this exclusivity from the position of their supposed purpose in creating a secure life. All these institutions or "systems" must be analyzed in terms of economic pedagogics.

In the first place, we must clearly understand the mechanism by which a system establishes these monopolies (teaching,

---

12 See Illich, *Libérer l'avenir,* 111.

health, transportation, etc). The "system" pretends to be the only pedagogical medium for completing its task. This is why such systems eliminate all pre-existing and parallel subsystems, meticulously annihilating all those seemingly necessary attempts to supplement the limits of the system. Take an example from biology. Antibiotics and intensive chemotherapy, which are so abusively present in the "healthcare system," have in some cases eliminated pathogens, but have also eliminated other subsystems of germs which are necessary in maintaining a patient's' physiological equilibrium. In this case the "antibiotic system" assumes the exclusive right to cure and goes on to destroy different kinds of "natural" systems which pre-exist antibiotics. The organism thus becomes vulnerable to many new diseases. What error could the irrational administration of chemotherapy have made? What is not taken into account is that the human organism itself, before the introduction of medicine, is truly, fundamentally, a "healthcare system." In the same way, the "school system" presumes that the child is totally ignorant, a *tabula rasa* (just as chemotherapy presumes that a sick person is totally sick: without any of her own defenses against sickness). The "school system" presumes the child is an orphan, without any kind of culture (because the *people's culture* is deemed nonexistent). The "school" thus assumes the grand task of delivering culture to the child (much as the doctor believes he gives health to the sick). In doing so, this "school system" eliminates educational subsystems, such as those that exist in family life, lessons from the community or neighborhood elders, and those from the priest or aunt—the people who educate the children around them. It not only eliminates the most inexpensive, real, and perfectly adapted mechanisms for educating the young in day-to-day life, but it critiques those processes as if they were its enemy (just like the doctor, rather than educating "healers," simply persecutes them as blasphemous shamans). Conclusion: the "system" becomes expensive, unique, and exclusive, and the community relinquishes its control over the education of its own people. Besides an enormous lack of responsibility, this also produces a significant distortion in this "systematic" education. This "system," in fact, does not educate the child. Rather it alienates him, steeping him in a culture that is not his own, a culture of the prevailing political, social, ideological, and other interests. The "education system's" bureaucracy serves this culture at any given moment.

The "systems" invent themselves, define themselves, grow and then defend themselves until they become like a cancer which no one can cure. "Only within limits can education fit people into a man-made environment: beyond these limits lies the universal schoolhouse, hospital ward, or prison."[13] Primary schools, secondary schools and universities, which are paid for by the community (since the physical equality to enter school hides the inequality of educational possibilities),[14] are used by the oligarchs, the national bourgeoisie and by the members of the "enlightened culture" in our dependent nations. The "system" therefore benefits those already learned and educated; those who need culture to secure their power. Because the "system" is an instrumental Totality, it possesses a mechanism which takes humans into its grip, and this is why

> future research ought to lead in the opposite direction (to that of current research); let us call it counterfoil research. Counterfoil research also has two major tasks: to provide guidelines for detecting the incipient stages of murderous logic in a tool (I would call it "logic of the Totality"); and to devise tools and tool systems that optimize the balance of life, thereby maximizing liberty for all [...]. The "educational system" is one of those carcinogenic systems.[15]

---

13 Illich, *Tools for Conviviality*, 6.
14 The child of a cultured family in our underdeveloped communities has advantages over an illiterate child. At the same time "[i]n medicine the same principle assures that suffering will increase with increased medical care; the rich will be given more treatment for iatrogenic diseases and the poor will just suffer from them" (ibid., 10).
15 Ibid., 3–46. The value of our author's reflections consist in indicating the contradiction of certain systems: they say they educate but they uneducate, they say they cure and they make sick, but, what is most important is that the "systems" themselves cannot be self-governed: "With the possible

The "productive institution" known as *school* delivers the "goods" denominated *education* to the public. This institution's deliverable is the *student*. Entangled in the web of the "knowledge economy," the student — who appears as its "consumer" — is not entirely satisfied, as evidenced by the student rebellions throughout fifty countries in 1969, according to reports by UNESCO. The educational system fulfills its purpose in all regards: it forms citizens that can genuinely serve the functions society assigns them. Beyond this lesson, nothing is worth learning. The "schooling system" is therefore rather like the "rite of initiation" of secular society. The "certificate" or the "diploma" are thus keys to secure a place within the system's purview. As we saw in chapter two of this book, modern education is nothing but a system to educate bourgeois, imperial and enlightened "man" in the colonies. "Schooling," such as one sees today, has been instrumental throughout the "periphery" (aside from China) in alienating children from communities to condition and instruct them in the *ethos* of a society constituted by international corporations; instructing them in an empire of money and violent competition. In Latin America "deschooling" is an urgently needed reform of the "school system."

Consider Law 19326, which was passed by the government of Peru in 1972. The law tells us that it attempts to

> awaken in Peruvians a *critical consciousness* of their situation and, consequently, adequately bring forth among them a just perspective on knowledge and action, actions which they ac-

---

exception of China under Mao, no present government could restructure society along convivial lines. The managers of our major tools — nations, corporations, parties, structured movements, professions-hold power. This power is vested in the maintenance of the growth-oriented structures which they manipulate. These managers have the power to make major decisions; they can generate new demands for the output of their tools and enforce the creation of new social labels to fit them. They can even go so far as to limit the output of tools in the interest of maximizing benefits. But they have no power to reverse the basic structure of the institutional arrangements which they manage [...]. Such an inversion of society is beyond the managers of present institutions" (23).

> complish as participants in the historical process of undoing structures of dependency and domination and as free men committed to the future of their country [...]. A communal education, founded in an educational community through dialogue and responsible participation.[16]

But this grand project needs other educational tools besides the "school," — as in the Chinese revolution, where all citizens were made to participate in educational activities. Thus

> it is necessary to overcome the exclusively school-based conception of education, so limited, rigid, and inadequate, and take a more integrated approach, recognizing the possibilities of other educative channels that are no less effective and sometimes providing a better influence than the school, like the family, distinct social grounds, and mass media, to cite the most important.[17]

We must therefore end the "age of school." The modern bourgeoisie began this age in Europe, defining it with Rousseau and his *Emile*.[18] It is truly a "pedagogical syndrome" which must be overcome, particularly in Latin America, that peripheral and dependent region where "school" is the system by which members of the people's culture become alienated and excluded from

---

16 *Law Decree 19326* or "General Law of Education," 10–11. In the *Informe General* [*General Report*] on "Peruvian educational reform," we read that "the traditional educational system in all its characteristics always reflected the nature of global society's system and decisively contributed to its perpetuation" (15); "exaggerating the end, we might say, even though without being completely misguided, that we are spending more than seven million to produce more illiterate people [...]. Educational shortcomings are compounded by social deformations and the economics of a dependent and alienated country, the most potent of these negative results from those of the national system of education" (16).

17 Ibid., 40.

18 See Illich, "L'école, cette vache sacrée" ["School, or The Sacred Cow"], in Illich, *Libérer l'avenir,* 120. For a repercussion in the European world on the question of "deschooling," see Hartmut von Hentig, *Cuernavaca oder Alernativen zur Schule?* (Munich: Klett/Koesel, 1971), 136–39.

high culture (leaving in their subjectivities a bitter taste of failure, while, at the same time, a guilty conscience for not being "enlightened," thereby passively accepting the State's neocolonial oppression of their people).

The "educational system," which begins with *schooling,* is elitist, despite the fact that it is obligatory and free of charge. This combination fully expresses its logic of domination in the universities, science and technology, and, lastly, and most extensively, in mass media.

"Right now, in Latin America, universities serve principally to maintain the institutional order of things, or, at most, the extent to which societies reflect modernization."[19] They are the culmination of the functionalist professionalization of education in a society headed towards consumerism, extreme neocolonial dependence, and the internalized learning of imperial culture thanks to its national oligarchs. The political system that secures neocolonial protection (thanks to its military apparatus) and underdevelopment (thanks to economic exploitation), produces with the university an alienated culture of the periphery. This is why the humanities are dangerous for the Empire, particularly sociology and psychology, which encourage the development of critical consciousness.[20] In general one might say that the highest costs in funding Latin American universities do not have corresponding returns, but this is because they have not been interpreted in light of their contributions to national and

---

19 Darcy Ribeiro, *La Universidad Latinoamericana* [*The Latin American University*] (Santiago: Editorial Universitaria, 1971), 100 (see the bibliography on pages 303–14). In addition to this text by Ribeiro—the most important in its genre—we should also mention his Darcy Ribeiro, *La Universidad Nueva: Un Proyecto* [*The New University: A Project*] (Venezuela: Fundacion Biblioteca Ayacucho, 1973).

20 See "Imperio, Universidad y CIA" ["Empire, University, and the CIA"], in Héctor Silva Michelena and Heinz Rudolf Sonntag, *Universidad, Dependencia y Revolución* [*University, Dependency and Revolution*] (Mexico: Siglo Veintiuno, 1971), 141–50. Regarding the question "Is a Sociology of Liberation Possible?" see Orlando Fals Borda, *Ciencia Propia y Colonialismo Intelectual* [*Hard Science and Intellectual Colonialism*] (Mexico: Nuestro Tiempo, 1970), 22–55.

social processes of liberation. Brain drain is one small indication of these frightful contradictions.

The complex formed by science and technology faces a similar situation. A long colonial and neocolonial history has left Latin America extremely dependent on science and technology from the "center."[21] But, what is worse, epistemological blindness prevents researchers from taking full responsibility for the politics of their science. Oscar Varsavsky has shown the inherent fallacy in thinking that the sciences access a "*universal* objectivity," as in physics and mathematics. The validity of this objectivity is always conditioned by economic and political forces which frequently go unnoticed by Latin American scientists:

> The loss of the developmentalist-scientistic illusion allows the general problem of science's mission in society to become politicized. We may come to the conclusion that it is directly involved in the process of replacing [society] with a better one [...] it is clear that by pleading against the current system leads to the acceptance of all the critiques raised by the rebel groups, in all countries and all ages.[22]

It is still true therefore that intellectuals' responsibility in the "center" is much more pressing, particularly in the United States and Europe, as Chomsky and Marcuse have noted.[23] Depend-

---

21 See Helio Jaguaribe, *Desarrollo Económico y Desarrollo Politico* [*Economic and Political Development*] (Buenos Aires: EUDEBA, 1964), 23–49; Amílcar Herrera, *Ciencia y Política en América Latina* [*Science and Politics in Latin America*] (Mexico: Siglo Veintiuno, 1971); and for a book on the "center," see Jean J. Salomon, *Ciencia y Política* [*Science and Politics*] (Mexico: Siglo Veintiuno, 1974), 265–77.

22 Oscar Varsavsky, *Ciencia, Política y Cientificismo* [*Science, Politics, and Scientificism*] (Buenos Aires: Capital Intelectual, 1971), 79–80. *La Revista Ciencia Nueva* (out of Buenos Aires) has included a good amount of critical material on this issue.

23 The profound origin of "radical" thought in the center has diverse beginnings. We will recount one of them. Before World War II, Edmund Husserl, *Die Krisis der europäische Wissenschaften* (The Hague: Nijhoff, 1962), 149, indicated the ontological priority of the "lifeworld" (*Lebenswelt*, that is, "what is given" or *Vorgegebenheit*): science is a thematic plane emerg-

ing from the non-thematic horizon of the quotidian. From this hypothesis, Martin Heidegger, *Die Frage nach dem Ding* (Tübingen: Niemeyer, 1962), 68, shows similarly that the question of the thing comes after the question of Being and of the world: science — since the Renaissance — assumes a natural comprehension. In this tradition, though mediated by the findings of the Frankfurt School, see Herbert Marcuse, *One-Dimensional Man* (New York: Routledge, 2013) (see part II, chapters 6 and 7, on technological rationality and positivism) [Translators' Note: Dussel did not provide the English citation here]. Noam Chomsky's *American Power and the New Mandarins* (London: Penguin Books, 2003) explicitly situates the problem of science, technology, and the "intellectual" in an ethical-political reflection starting from the war in Vietnam. Chomsky offers an x-ray of the intellectual "warrior": "The *intelligentsia*'s new technical access to power: Is an illusion or an increasing reality? (26). Thus begins the critique of *universality*'s pretend *objectivity* in the sciences. On the other hand, there is something called the "human sciences" which begin to discover their ethical-political priority over the "natural sciences" (be them exact or factical). See Stephan Strasser, *Phénoménologie et sciences de l'homme* (Louvain: Nauwelaerts, 1967). Another aspect of the redefinition of science, technology, and the function given to the intellectual from the "center" may be found in Antonio Gramsci's thought, Antonio Gramsci, "The Formation of Intellectuals," in *Selections from the Prison Notebooks*, ed. and trans. Quentin Hoare and Geoffrey Nowell Smith (New York: International Publishers, 1971), 3–23, which tells us that "[t]he mode of being of the new intellectual can no longer consist in eloquence, which is an exterior and momentary mover of feelings and passions, but in active participation in practical life, as constructor, organizer, 'permanent persuader' and not just a simple orator (but superior at the same time to the abstract mathematical spirit); from technique-as-work one proceeds to technique-as-science and to the humanistic conception of history, without which one remains 'specialized' and does not become 'directive' (specialized and political)" (10). Gramsci thinks that the intellectual can be revolutionary if they are organically united with the community. For the periphery, see Mao Tse-tung's thinking, "Recruit Large Numbers of Intellectuals," in *Selected Works of Mao Tse-tung*, vol. II (Peking: Foreign Languages Press, 1967) 301–3, where he declares that "[w]ithout the participation of the intellectuals victory in the revolution is impossible." We have seen that neocolonial imperialism first eliminates the intellectuals; this is the case in Brazil, Chile, Zaire, or Czechoslovakia. Those in the "human sciences," the liberatory critics, are persecuted in particular. The best "work horse" the center has to complete its domination is therefore scientific positivism (see Ernest Gellner, "Review of Theodor W. Adorno et al., "The Positivist Dispute in German Sociology," *British Journal for the Philosophy of Science* 34, no. 2 [1983]: 173–75), because it wants to have — to a structured epistemological extent — total moral, political, and human interpolation: its fake "objectivity" transforms itself into an "innocent" weapon.

ence on technology is the subtlest and imprisoning of dependences: it is how the technological basis of community development in the periphery becomes dominated.

But the "educational system" does not stop at the school. It continues with what we can call the "community's university": mass media. First among them is radio (which can reach the illiterate, as well as remote locations across economic levels), next is television (growing in Latin American viewership), which is followed by newspapers, magazines, books, propaganda, etc. About 80% of this entire "system" of collective communication in our dependent Latin America *belongs* to the United States (directly, through sole or principal shareholders of giant companies; or indirectly, through control of news agencies and propaganda, etc). Most disquieting in this situation is not who owns and maintains the mechanisms of this industry, but rather the invisible manipulation of its "ideological syndrome." Essentially the "system of communication" promotes *a market*. The totality of the Latin American population is considered (just like *Emile*) as a *tabula rasa*, with neither culture nor history (in other words, as an orphan).[24] It becomes a population without its own needs, without culturally-appropriate responses, without relevance. The mass media "express" electronically formulated models of propaganda and they "create" the desire to consume goods produced by countries in the "center." This "ideological syndrome" has a unique mechanism. In the first place, the "objects" it introduces to the viewer's knowledge (beverage n, cigarette x, perfume z) are neutral objects, without ethical or political value. The mechanism plays upon an image of becoming more of a man or woman, more modern, more beautiful. But at the same time it promotes the introjection of the system, because the most modern person [graph is here] will be more successful in business or in conquering the most beautiful woman (like the sense, taught through propaganda, that one is "in the money"). *Competition,* the victory of the strongest, as distinct

---

24 See "La Dependencia Tecnológica" ["Techno-dependency"], in Silva and Sonntag, *Universidad, Dependencia y Revolución*, 135–40.

interactions (like in cowboy movies, or superhero stories like Superman and Batman), equally introduces an *ethos* of violence rather than an ethos of justice. Thus the public *wants* what the media puts in front of them, instructing their intuitions *pedagogically*. The media is a "community school," though it is not managed by teachers, officials, or neocolonial States. Rather, this "community school's" administration are the largest multinational corporations, in service of the imperial culture and in collaboration with the neocolonial elite's high culture. Both of these cultures agree that the new, national, liberated people's culture must be unraveled.[25]

There are other *pedagogical* "systems" such as, for example, the "healthcare system" which does not teach the community how to treat its own illnesses and prevent sickness, but rather attacks symptoms with unilateral violence, as in surgery or chemotherapy. This healthcare system teaches the public, like Rousseau in *Emile*, that only doctors know about disease and so their diagnoses must be followed blindly. The healthcare system teaches the public to obey its every command and not to try and understand its mystery, since that encourages the dangerous quackery of folk medicine and other types of mumbo-jumbo at odds with scientific rationality and the doctor's art. In this way, "the capitalism of knowledge, inherent in professional imperialism, subjugates the people in an imperceptible way; which is just as effective as weapons or international finance."[26] This quality is

---

[25] The same way that the Cartesian cogito is originally empty of contents, apparently being part of its proper fundament; also for Newton, the fact that space is empty and absolute is axiomatic in physics. Similarly, economics begin with an "empty market" that becomes full of "merchants" that sell things to some universal, ideal, and pure consumer.

[26] See Armand Mattelart, *La Comunicación Masiva en el Proceso de Liberación* [*Mass Communication in the Process of Liberation*] (Buenos Aires: Siglo Veintiuno, 1973), 43, who explains that "the object, the new fetish, masks a class which brandishes its political utopia of civic equality among men to proclaim a pragmatic democracy through consumption and production. Like the aphorism on a television commercial says: TV is for everyone and everyone loves brand X." See also M.J. McLuhan and Quentin Fiore, *War and Peace in the Global Village* (Toronto: Penguin, 2003).

most notable in the doctor's pedagogical liturgy, making himself loved by those he dominates and exploits. On this subject we can conclude that

> First, health care has less impact on health than is generally supposed; second, compared with a different set of socio-environmental variables, modern medical care has less impact on health that many of these factors (food, care, etc.); third, and finally, given the direction in which our society is evolving and evolutionary imperatives within the same health system, future medical care will have even less effect than it does now.[27]

This is the *death of medicine,* which began only two centuries ago, like the ongoing death of the school.[28]

We must therefore make a new school, a new medicine, and other new services for the oppressed. To do this, it is necessary to first demystify imperial pedagogics, show its disproportionate costs, and finally point towards a more liberatory path.

---

27 Illich, *Tools for Conviviality,* 47. For bibliography on the topic, see 42.

28 Carlson, *Limits of Medicine,* 154. Carlson describes "The End of Medicine" as a transition to "[a] macro-medicine" (61–182). It is interesting to note that the old are particularly "exploited" by chemotherapeutic and clinical-hospital industry, through the doctor, as in the US. In 1970 every person over 65 years spent $791 (annually), and only 296 of those 19 to 65 years old reached that figure. The "old" (the countries of the "center" have high retirements) are the preferred medicinal object (6, 104ff). It would be very interesting to take other cases of "educational systems" as, for example, transportation as currently practiced: all traditional and very cheap, like the bicycle, horse, etc., are suppressed in favor of the automobile and the consumer oil of large multinational companies (both cars and extraction and marketing of oil). See Illich, *Alternatives to Transportation,* 44: "the typical American devotes more than 1,500 hours per year to his car: sitting in it, going to work or stopped, working in order to pay for gas, tires, tolls, insurance, infringements and federal taxes for roads and parking." And, worst of all, this trend makes us believe the "peripheral" countries do not enjoy the benefits of owning their own car. We are taught to buy a car and drive it to save time ("because it's gold"), but at the same time cars produce difficulties in growing cities. It is more difficult to live with one's family and get to work today than it was during colonial Christendom.

52

Ethics of the Pedagogical Pro-ject

Economics studies the *distance* mediating the face-to-face, while pedagogics studies that which freely nourishes, clothes and shelters—like a gift of being. Yet play and learning are a *proto-economic;* they are pre-work, a preparation for "service" or a preparation for the praxis of domination. Those who become oppressors, oppressed, and liberators do so within a pedagogical temporality. Does everything depend on the "pedagogical methods" used? No. But, everything does definitively depend on each pedagogical system's *pro-ject*. We know that the project is the foundation of ontology, whether it is the present being of a Totality (the reigning totality) or that of a Totality to come (the pro-ject of liberation).[1] We also know that *ethics* refers to the meta-physical project of the Other (while morality is merely the ontic relation of behavior to law, whether present or yet-to-come). Thus, we claim that the ethics of the pedagogical pro-ject entails a consideration of whether the aim of education negates the child–community or affirms its authentic exteriority. Making such a claim requires judging the pro-jects inherent in pedagogical systems, their basic objectives, and the ultimate

---

1   See Enrique Dussel, *Para una Ética de la Liberación Latinoamericana, Book I*, sections 2–6, 21–22, 46, 58.

ends of education. In general, pedagogues and educational researchers are technocrats, bureaucratic curriculum builders for the system. They neither think about, nor question, the ultimate pro-ject of the system they build, which is essential. We must keep these systems' intents clearly in mind. This is especially important in Latin America, where the predominant systems aim towards the "center's" imperial cultural pro-ject (by which we mean almost exclusively European and North American culture, and the 3% of our population clearly influenced by Russia). Furthermore, in these prevailing systems, the elite oligarchs confuse their real pedagogical pro-ject with that of the "center," negating — as we see in Sarmiento — the pro-ject of the people's culture. The poet tells us that

> you must fight against everyone, and your fight will be sad because you will struggle against your own blood. Your father will never recognize you. You will be a dark son — Malinche cries to her mestizo son —; [Europe] will never see you as anything but its slave; you will have to recognize your orphanity...[2]

In this section we must bring precise clarity to certain notions which are often confused. We will try to clarify the following (each of which includes its own fundamental pro-ject): *imperial culture*, or the self-proclaimed "universal" culture, *national culture* (which is not the same as the people's culture), *high culture* of the neocolonial elite (which, while not always bourgeois, is always oligarchical), *popular culture* (which is equally alienating and one-dimensional for both the "center" and the "periphery"), and finally *the people's culture*.[3]

---

[2] Carlos Fuentes, "Todos los Gatos son Pardos" ["All Cats are Brown"], in *Los Reinos Originarios* [*The Original Kingdoms*] (Paris: French & European Publications, Inc., 1971), 23–195, at 115.

[3] With respect to notions such as the imperial State, neocolonial State, nation, country, and especially community, see *Para una Ética de la Liberación Latinoamericana*, sections 55–56.

Imperial culture, high culture, and popular culture (which must include workers' culture-as-negativity) are moments of the prevailing system, the dominant pedagogical Totality. Though it is misleading, national culture is an important category. Whether the culture of a "dominating" nation or that of a "peripheral" nation, national culture serves to mediate the developing countries' understanding of what national liberation is, though that understanding may be contradictory. Essentially, the people's culture is the key concept in the "pedagogics of liberation." This pedagogics' pro-ject is exclusively liberatory, ethically just, humanizing, and alterative. Such a pedagogics of liberation is rooted in those cultures which child finds at home and when interacting with her parents.

As we will see, there is a pro-ject contrary to the humanizing pro-ject just mentioned, which seeks to totalize the child. This is the ethically perverse pro-ject of *domination* which anticipates the imperial pedagogical pro-ject (where the father-dominator extends the domination of his own child to other fathers' children). There exists another pro-ject as well: that of the *liberation of the child*. This *liberatory* pedagogical pro-ject lets the child exist in its birth-reality (which is the liberatory position of the new State towards the oppressed, where the State is respectful of their alterity). We will describe this pedagogics of liberation at both the erotic-domestic level as well as the political level, as we have done throughout this book. We will conclude that the latter has a particular significance for Latin America, given the many valid analogical norms pedagogy and evolutionary psychology offer the child of the "center" and the child of the "periphery."

In this chapter and the next, we will undertake an exposition of Figure 4, below.

First, observe line (b), which represents how *the pedagogical pro-ject can be defined by dominance*. By "pedagogical pro-ject defined by dominance" we mean an understanding of the dominating group in its historical and concrete being (whether "center," class, father, teacher, etc.). In this case the child–community is taught "the Same," inherent as it is in the existing system. Thus the pedagogical pro-ject of domination is always

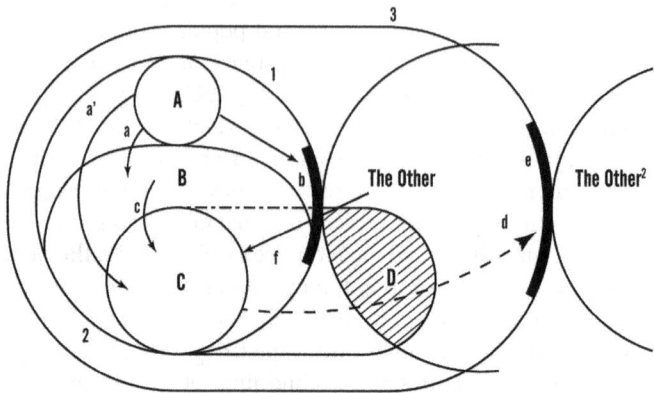

Figure 4. Pedagogical pro-jects of domination and liberation: different levels of culture and cultural praxis. 1: Imperial pedagogical totality; A: "center"; a: praxis of domination from center to periphery; b: pro-ject of domination; 2: peripheral pedagogical subtotality; B: dependent oligarchy; c: intranational, dependant praxis of subdomination; C-D: community; C: the oppressed in a community; D: the community as exteriority; d: praxis of liberation; e: pro-ject of liberatory pedagogics; f: pedagogical interpellation from exteriority (In the erotic-domestic pedagogical background: 1: the family; A: the father; 2: maternal-filial totalization; B: the mother; C-D: the child; C: the child as oppressed; D: the child as exteriority).

the result of violence, conquest, and repression of the Other as other. Politically, the pedagogics of domination is the result of a bureaucratic ossification and aging of social structure; in other words, the gerontocracy.[4] This is similar to what Spengler would

---

4   We have indicated the social-psychoanalytic analysis of Pierre Legendre, *L'amour du censeur: Essai sur l'ordre dogmatique* (Paris: Seuil, 1974), addressing the pontifical and canonical right in the Middle Ages where the author shows the origin of this actual occidental administrative right. It is keen to show "institutions" in relation to the Freudian interpretation of self-censorship (*Über-Ich*). Schumpeter explains that "[t]he bureaucracies of Europe, in spite of the fact that they have drawn enough hostile criticism to blur their records, exemplify very well what I am trying to convey. They are the product of a long development that started with the administrations of medieval magnates (originally serfs selected for administrative and mili-

call "civilization," as the fossilization of cultural production processes.[5] Present culture — as we have defined it elsewhere[6] — is the organic conjunction of predetermined dispositions through attitudes (*ethos*) in the face of technology (civilization), whose teleological instance is constituted by values and symbols belonging to the group engaged in an ontological project. In other words, the present culture is composed of lifestyles which manifest in production and transform the non-built environment into a world sponsored by the dominant culture. This reigning *totality* of symbolic mediations is the basic architecture of a pedagogics of domination's pro-ject (*b* in Figure 4). Since the present culture is *reigning* and *dominant,* political power commands the totality of the population in that given system. If we are speaking of the entire geopolitical milieu within which the empire exercises its predominance, then it is an *imperial* culture (A in Figure 4). This culture (which today is European-Russian-American) (A) imposes itself upon the peripheral milieus and thereby dominates their *national* cultures (totality 2 in Figure

---

tary purposes who thereby acquired the status of petty nobles) and went on through the centuries until the powerful engine emerged which we behold today" (Joseph A. Schumpeter, *Capitalism, Socialism, and Democracy* [New York: Harper, 1950], 294). Bureaucratic management of pedagogy (like everything that falls into its hands, as Henry Kissinger showed in the chapter "The Impact of Administrative Structure" in his book *American Foreign Policy* (New York: Norton, 1977), constitutes the teacher in an "employment" lacking in all creativity and exposed day-to-day to inspectors working with a cold and distant design. Teacher and child thus introject the social censure of programs and laws, the Freudian superego, which obligates us with steely urgency and pseudo-morals. The "bureaucratic mechanism" is an essential part of dominant pedagogy.

5 See Herbert Marcuse, "Remarks on a Redefinition of Culture," in *The Essential Marcuse: Selected Writings of Philosopher and Social Critic Herbert Marcuse,* eds. Andrew Feenberg and William Leiss (Boston: Beacon, 2007), 13–31. We are therefore in disagreement with Marcuse (and the Frankfurt School) when they speak of "superior culture" as the best, as opposed to the trendy culture which is "prevailing, political, and popular" (14). The "intellectual elite" remains poorly defined, as well as the people's culture.

6 See Enrique Dussel, "Latin American Culture," in *A History of the Church in Latin America: Colonialism to Liberation (1492–1979),* trans. Alan Neely (Michigan: William B. Eerdmans Publishing Company, 1981), 21–31, at 23.

4). A rift forms within these peripheral, neocolonial States. On the one hand, an alienated culture emerges imitating that of the center. Its "center" is therefore outside its borders, and the resulting culture is *high* culture (B) which dominates what we may call *popular culture* (C). The way in which popular culture is dominated happens in a double sense: first, it is dominated directly (a') (by a television show in Spanish produced in Miami, for example), or mediated by neocolonial oligarchs (c). We must realize that popular culture (C) is not the exteriority of the *people's culture* properly speaking, though the community concretely composes each of these cultures (since the community contains values, symbols, and habits of the introjected system [C] and other distinct values, symbols, and habits [D]).

We should make two other observations. First, every reigning culture (whether it be imperial culture or high culture) has always been the result of a creative process which the people drive. The European-American bourgeois culture was the result of a long campaign waged against the feudal, rural, and Christian world by the bourgeoisie which lasted nearly a thousand years. The high culture of the oligarchs is also the result of a people's movement in the Creole community. In Latin America, for another example, such a movement rose against the Spanish bureaucracy's monopoly on symbols (whose viceroys', judges', etc., salaries came from Spain). In the wake of this people's movement, however, the people's creativity divides and *cultural domination* appears, both in imperial and oligarchical form. Thus the difference between popular culture and the people's culture. Second, popular culture in the "center" can be as dominant, or even more dominant, than in the "periphery." This is because popular culture in the "periphery" has experienced its exteriority (D), whereas the "center's" popular culture has been totally included within the reigning culture's system. Thus the world-wide cultural revolution must always arise from the oppressed of the "periphery."

Just as the father dominates his child with "the Same," the state dominates its people. One separates the child from its mother, the other separates the people from its culture and exteriority. This is why the "periphery's" national culture (like the oppressed family, so different from the dominating oligarch's family) is a living contradiction, a situation Hegel would call "civil society."[7] The contradiction has two faces. The first is an oligarchy which presents itself through imperial culture as the "superior" and "universal" culture, the culture which is worthy of study and to which one must travel (oligarchical tourism's Mecca is Europe). The second face of the contradiction presents itself through an exteriority (D), through its distinct values and original customs (whose travels lead one to Machu Picchu, the legendary Tikal in Guatemala, or Mount Albán in Oaxaca). Combining alienating high culture and the authentic people's culture-as-exteriority, results in an amorphous and bastardized popular culture in which both the "cultured" elite as well as the people themselves participate. This popular culture is the *universal* or *unequivocal identity* which wields a power, rooted as it is in a strategic ideology delivered by pedagogical mechanisms that manipulate public opinion.[8]

The way we intend to use the word "ideology" is different than the one so in vogue today.[9] By "ideology" we mean the practico-operative and existential *interpretive totality*. Hermeneutics is the act of discovering meaning. But any particular meaning is a single instance within a totality of meaning, which is the world. The world opens itself, or becomes comprehensible, through the horizon of being: the pro-ject. Through projects we come to com-prehend the potentiality of being (*telos*), grounding our ability to interpret this or that thing *in a particular way*. Interpretation as an act of subjectivity draws relations between meaning and project. Yet if a pro-ject is sponsored by

---

7   For an explanation, see *Para una Ética de la Liberación Latinoamericana*, section 55.
8   See a European "state of the question" of the problematic of ideology in the co-organized book edited by Hans Lieber with the participation of Horkheimer, Marcuse, Tillich, Plessner, et al.: Hans Lieber, *Ideologienlehre und Wissenssoziologie: Die Diskussion um das Ideologieproblem in den zwanziger Jahren* (Darmstadt: Wissenschaftliche Buchgesellschaft, 1974).
9   See sections 65–69 of *Para una Ética de la Liberación Latinoamericana*.

the dominant culture, that pro-ject closes Totality off to Alterity (the child and the people-as-Other, historically speaking). Such a project can no longer discover its real potentiality of being, and thus becomes unreal, schizophrenic, totalized, perverse, and dead. Reality, the meaning of things, is hidden from such a fixed totality. False interpretations of meanings emerge when one's world-horizon promotes this very unreality. False attribution of sense to an ambiguous word and uttering discourses which mask other discourses: these are examples of false interpretation. The thing itself, "that which appears," the phenomenon, transforms into mere appearance, false presence, and concealment. Speech becomes gossip[10]: a living metonymic chain of words only signifying other words, people talking about talking just to talk. Desire to know true reality turns into capricious curiosity, a desire to know about novelties as mere novelties without searching for newness, and thus becoming enveloped within a novelty without newness. The mysterious exteriority which distinguishes each person becomes rooted in conformity. Triviality becomes king, as propaganda, *kitsch,* trendiness. "Modern and imported" goods, used up stuff, all meaningless, come to dominate the "mass man's" world. His values, symbols, conduct, and pro-ject form the totality of *popular culture.* The one-dimensionality with which we must interpret Donald Duck and Patoruzú is the same one-dimensionality with which sports fans enjoy their games. In them, we see the specter of a universal culture steeped in the ideology of the "center." We must therefore clearly distinguish the *unequivocal universality* of the culture produced in the "center" from *analogical worldliness.* The latter (always in mortal danger and at the precipice of violation, vulnerable to imperial domination and universal

---

10 See Martin Heidegger, *Sein und Zeit* (Tübingen: Max Niemeyer, 1977), 167. Heidegger describes the inauthentic "quotidian being [*alltägliches Sein*]." The danger in this is that Europeans do not come to distinguish between inauthentic popular culture and authentic people's culture. The only "exit" will be the tragedy of critical-elitism of the few sages that separate the mass-community via critique. This is an inadequate solution of the intellectual-history relation.

counter-revolutionary manipulation) is inherent in that culture which must break forth, liberating the peoples' cultures of every "peripheral" country (Latin American culture, Islamic culture, African culture, Indian culture, Chinese culture, and Southeast Asian culture).

The ideological mechanisms of imperial pedagogics are highly efficient and effective because they pose as "natural." Imperial and universal culture's message is tautological: it always talks about the "the Same," repeating this theme in different ways *ad infinitum*. One's sense of listening, watching, and memory are bombarded by text, image, and the same flattened meaning of each thing. The imperial message is so universally present in everything that it becomes disingenuous not to accept it because it is so obvious. Non-critique becomes subjectivity's normal pedestrian mode of being in the world. And of course, losing one's position in the social order is dangerous. It is a grave risk, which is what will happen if one gives a different meaning to something. Being distinct is grounds for persecution. Questioning the historical and political origins of things is bad taste and bad behavior in this culture. This kind of provocation is considered *vulgar culture, i*n the eyes of imperial culture, high culture, and popular-consumer culture (*vulgar* being a demeaning term which lets the former negate, annihilate, and muddle authentic *people's culture*). The vulgate is heterogeneous irrationality, uncultured barbarism, Greek *hubris,* "the masses" (*hoi polloi*) devalued by Heraclitus and Hegel (his *Vielheit*). That which is rude, uneducated, rough, vulgar, shocking, is identified as being of the people (D in figure 2). Imperial ideology has an interest in keeping the people dangerous because

> there has always been a "foreign" universe to which the cultural goals were not applied: the Enemy, the Other, the Alien, the Outcast — terms referring not primarily to individuals but to groups, religions, "ways of life," social systems. In meeting the Enemy (who has his epiphany also within one's

own universe) culture is suspended or even prohibited, and inhumanity can often run its course.[11]

The subject of imperial ideology, teacher of pop-cultural pedagogy, uses a language that goes beyond tautology and puts everything under a kind of spell (religious, romantic, festive or childish music composed to "sell" a product). At the same time this language is authoritative ("buy now!" and "vote!"), in an environment of false familiarity ("this is your facial cream," "your supermarket"). This ideological language is a language of immediacy: its facthood cannot be rebutted, and imposes itself with its own reason. The thing is confused with its own function, its truth is status quo truth. "The Same" invades everything. Semantic relations become tautological because the signifiers intended to give meaning to things in the world are concepts for everyone to interpret in everyday speech. Linguistic signifiers are now text communications, and anyone using them understands their meaning. The circuit of communication from sender to receiver, through which signifiers pass, yields certain pieces of information to those same channels. Receiving the information entails the same set of codes (phonetics, syntax, semantics) along with the same systems of decodification. Imperial cultures "use" the linguistic-ideological totality like a pedagogical tool on the people in order to transform it into popular culture, a manageable cultural mass. "Culture," or being educated (the "school system" established for this latter purpose), is defined by its ability to adequately receive and manage the channels (television, radio, newspapers, magazines, etc.) and the codes (alphabet, speech, paralanguage, etc.) through the fixed structures of which ("figures" in a children's cartoon, for instance) dominant and alienating information is introjected. The people will be taught to

---

[11] Marcuse, *The Essential Marcuse*, 15. Marcuse, who has noted the question of exteriority in many of his writings, does not know how to initiate the totality of his discourse from exteriority. He only indicates here or there, but nothing from the heart of his thinking: Here is his limit! The CIA's actions stem from an ideology of the "Other as Enemy." See also Víctor Marchetti and John Marks, *CIA and the Cult of Intelligence* (New York: Knopf, 1974).

become the mass. The creative and exteriorized people's culture is reduced to *kitsch,* massified substitutes and poor imitations of the real thing. Clearly this imperial culture is not innocent. Ideology concealed within the people's culture infuses a "system" into that culture which is not only intellectual but also erotic, political, and economic. We cannot be astonished by

> the time when capitalist imperialism takes hold of the totality of its resources. During this time the selection of workers is hurried, and their work — whether by belt or chain — tries with incredible might to adjust itself to systemized movement. At this point, the school was swept away by the current. In order to give a picturesque expression of our interpretation we can say that Ford, rather than Comenius, lies at the basis of the new technique (or technology) of school work. And it is natural that this is so: Comenius' *Didáctica Magna* corresponded to the manufacturing era of capitalism; the Decroly or Montessori system corresponds to imperial capitalism.[12]

Or, in other words:

> The vicissitudes of the language have their parallel in the vicissitudes of political behavior. In the sale of equipment for relaxing entertainment in bomb shelters, in the television show of competing candidates for national leadership, the juncture between politics, business, and fun is complete. But the juncture is fraudulent and fatally premature — business and fun are still the politics of domination… And again, it will not be the hero but the people who will be the ritual victims.[13]

---

12 Aníbal Ponce, *Educación y la Lucha de Clases* [*Education and Class Struggle*] (Buenos Aires: Materia, 1957), 268

13 Marcuse, *One-Dimensional Man,* 107.

Yet one more variable emerges in neocolonial or peripheral cultures. From within an imperial culture (like that of Spykmann) or high culture (like that of Sarmiento), a hybrid emerges that, despite its hybrid status, leans more towards the imperial culture than a dependent national culture. The bourgeois business elite in the national periphery, when present, has a form of high culture which is also national. Contrarily, what we might call this *managerial culture,* has

> rejected any notion of sovereignty and nation and stems from the ideology of multiplying the profits of international monopolies [...]. They are technocrats, business managers, rationalizing market researchers linking their own destiny to companies that extend from Argentina or Brazil to the United States or Israel without any distinguishing features.[14]

All of the above may be understood as constituting the dependent quality of a neocolonial national culture which has built up the dominating imperial culture. Internally, a contradictory rift forms within this national culture. First, it houses the anti-national, pro-empire managerial culture. Second, it contains the national bourgeoisie's high culture and those in solidarity with them. Third, popular culture imposes itself blatantly on the totality of the country's general population. This entire system of cultural dependence engenders a traditionalist and conservative attitude (we call it traditionalist and not traditional, because that which is traditional is always creative and belongs to the people). It appears as "old" culture in contrast to the innovative, chaotic, and subversive culture, but in reality, as we will see, this culture is actually the most traditional. The traditionalist attitude within the culture of dependence says that "everything was better in the past," in the sense that the oligarchs (who rose to power through a prior processes of liberation driven by the

---

14 Guillermo Gutiérrez, *Ciencia, Cultura y Dependencia* [*Science, Culture, and Dependency*] (Buenos Aires: Guadalupe, 1973), 33. This text introduces many of the distinctions we use here in this short presentation of culture.

people) see the future horizon of novelty closing in on them. They are destined to repeat the model that brought them to life, or they perish. Traditionalism in a culture of national dependence is merely another repetition of "the Same," a living death.

The pedagogical pro-ject of domination — ontological and existential horizon — cannot be conceptualized, thought, nor denoted properly speaking. As we have repeatedly indicated, it is pre-conceptual. However, we can reformulate it — from a clear and intelligible horizon — as a *pedagogical pro-ject* (which is ontic at this stage) which must be distinguished from the notion of a *pedagogical model*.[15] By pro-ject, we draw from what the phenomenologists of axiological ethics called an "ideal." Max Scheler explained that

> an ought becomes a moral and genuine ought whenever it is based on insight into objective values — i.e., in this context, into the morally good — there is also the possibility of an evidential insight into a good whose objective essence and value-content contain a reference to an individual person, and whose ought therefore comes to this person and to him as a "call," no matter if this "call" is addressed to others or not.[16]

What happens is that "objective values" can constitute a total system of dominant values: perverse as the totality and sublime in their particularity. What could be better than courage? What could be worse than the courage of an unjust conquistador?

---

15 Regarding the difference between pro-ject, project, and model, see section 58 of *Para una Ética de la Liberación Latinoamericana*.
16 Max Scheler, *Der Formalismus in der Ethik: Neuer Versuch der Grundlegung eines ethischen Personalismus* (Bern: Francke, 1954), 495. On this type of proposal see Eduard Spranger, "El Ideal Personal" ["The Personal Ideal"], in *Formas de Vida* [*Forms of life*] (Madrid: Revistas de Occidente, 1966), 406–42. English: Eduard Spranger, *Types of Men: The Psychology and Ethics of Personality*, trans. Paul John William Pigors (Halle: Niemeyer, 1928). His axiology does not accept that the ontological pro-ject is based on ideal structure of values. For more on this, see *Para una Ética de la Liberación Latinoamericana*, section 8.

In Latin America, educational policy and curricula articulate pedagogical *projects*. These political-pedagogical projects point to global trends, which states then commit to following. Such projects are implemented by inherently ideological *models*. In other words, we must understand and clarify the interpretive totality within which these models exist, the futures they hide, and the paths they open up.

Governments opting for dependence upon capitalism, supported by military force, promote a particular pedagogical project and model, for instance (think of Brazil, Chile, Bolivia in 1974, and the similar situations of Nicaragua, Haiti, etc). The model in these countries is domination: an authoritarianism which prioritizes the pedagogical system without critique, or what Paulo Freire calls "banking education." Science is scientism in these countries: an intellectual attitude where economics, politics, and social science pretend to discover universal values. Science and technology in these countries must be dependent on the "center." Just as such fake sciences think the critical spirit is essentially chaotic, subversive, and immoral, they eliminate the critical human sciences and legitimate exact sciences, such as natural science and technology; though they always do so with the aforementioned acritical and disingenuous "scientistic" spirit. Elementary school, secondary school, technical training, universities, mass media, propaganda, etc., all of them give credence to the tautological and authoritarian character of this intellectual attitude. Such a pedagogical pro-ject must imitate the imperial culture, introjecting empire and living in-step with it as an alienated culture of the masses, under the gerontocracy's thumb (which the very same nationalist culture of the bourgeoisie fought against for the people's culture). Latin America has undergone, in just this way, an accelerated "Americanization" of everyday life. This phenomenon transcends pedagogical regimes, and nowhere has it been more patently obvious than in Mexico, Central America, the Caribbean, and northern South America (principally Venezuela and Colombia). The empire's presence in our daily life signifies, in the short term, the annihilation of Latin America-as-cultural expression and the pre-

ETHICS OF THE PEDAGOGICAL PRO-JECT

vention of political-pedagogical action involving national liberation.

In the same way, the pedagogical system created by conservative-liberal models and blatant political-economic dependence (Colombia being the case in point) are not as authoritarian as the previous model. However, the people's education does not go beyond a system that teaches how to navigate the channels and signifiers of imperial language and its teachings, a system mediated by dominance. Critical education has barely advanced in these areas, if at all.

Thus the child, the people, and youth itself die. The people's culture introjects imperial culture, via managerial culture, through a process of repressive censure. The repression is pedagogical, psychological, political, and militarized. Its censure functions with a complex, high-level rationalization and coherence on the erotic domain of the family as well as on the political, commercial, and pedagogical domains. It is a "system" founded on a pedagogical pro-ject for which schooling is a decisive moment.

However, *the pedagogical pro-ject can also be liberatory* (*e* in Figure 4). An education that dominates is aggressive,[17] patriarchal, and authoritarian. It commits filicide. Liberatory education on the other hand "deploys the child's creative forces,"[18] as well as those of youth itself and the people. A liberatory project is one where the father respects the child's alterity. Just as Bartolomé de Las Casas admires the beauty, goodness, and culture of Indigenous peoples (the new, the Other), the father respects the child's new history. Similarly, revolutionary and insurgent governments taking power in a moment of social transformation educate the people while keeping its exteriority in mind (area *D* in Figure 4). The liberatory educational pro-ject is a future-oriented pro-ject, one which treats the oppressed as outside the

---

17 See the small book by Siegfried Keil, *Aggression und Mitmenschlichkeit* (Stuttgart: Kreuz, 1970).
18 Martin Buber, *Reden über Erziehung* (Heidelberg: Schneider, 1964), 11. See also Reinhold Mayer, *Franz Rosenzweig: Eine Philosophie der dialogischen Erfahrung* (Darmstadt: Buchsgesell, 1973).

present system. The people (simultaneously depicted as mass C and exteriority D) experience their own worlds as surpassing (in D) that system's horizon. Their "eschatological precipice" has its own demands, which form a totality rooted in a particular historical understanding of being that is advental and future-facing. This understanding does not merely comprehend the oppressed as a mass, but rather understands the people-as-exteriority and thus constitutes a liberatory pedagogics for the *people's culture.*

This people's culture forms an ineradicable and incorruptible center for resistance movements against oppression (for neocolonial nations as well as marginalized social classes). The people's culture is national culture's highest moment of authenticity. The antithesis of people's culture is popular culture, introjected as it is from oppressive systems. The people's culture operates in Latin America as one front of the war against oligarchy. First, it must fight the Spanish bureaucracy and its liberals, and then it must face national oligarchy, the bourgeoisie management class, and its imperial culture. The people's culture is the *real* culture, one composed of the symbols and structures found "at home." Historically, its artwork is made by the people, for the people, and expresses their creative processes. Their artwork is not "rustic" but rather the work of artisans, properly speaking. Music in particular tells the people's history, their trials and tribulations, through rhythm and words. Music is a kind of language, with its own structures, modes, and usages; a folklore that is more than folklore; traditions of events, "traditional" in its most authentic sense, referring to a set of symbols that express the people's plethora of forms and rituals. These symbols can include religious symbols animated by ancient communal wisdom explaining their origins. The traditional symbols can also include political symbols by which the community remembers its battles, heroes, traitors, friends, and enemies (typically communicated orally, without writing). Phenomenologists of religion call this kind of memory *super-historical.* The people's culture forms a totality of human meaning, largely *outside* the empire's pedagogical system.

We must not confuse the people's culture with mere folklore, however. And neither should we confuse it with Trotsky's proletarian culture, because the latter is a part of popular culture — or, in the best case, only part of the people's culture. The proletariat becomes defined within the industrial, capitalist, competitive system. Its exteriority is less, for example, than that of the field worker or of the marginalized. Proletariat culture in Latin America tends to fall under consumerism and, hence, it must defend its rights within the system (therefore defending the system itself) against society's most oppressed classes: the farmhand, the marginalized people, etc. The people's culture is also different from Oscar Lewis's culture of poverty — a mere moment of marginalized culture. In a culture of poverty, the people's culture is buried further down. In any case, each of these notions must be incorporated into a study or theory of culture from the periphery, but always with the central category of *people's culture.*

One pedagogical leader from the Third World, (whom, we should note, was an elementary school teacher before he was a political and military leader) explains that

> It is imperative to separate the fine old culture of the people which had a more or less democratic and revolutionary character from all the decadence of the old feudal ruling class [oligarchical culture...]. China's present new politics and new economy have developed out of her old politics and old economy, and her present new culture, too, has developed out of her old culture; therefore, we must respect our own history and must not lop it off. However, respect for history means giving it its proper place as a science, respecting its dialectical development [...]. As far as the masses and the young students are concerned, the essential thing is to guide them to look forward [pedagogical pro-ject of liberation] and not backward [imperial-oligarchical pro-ject].[19]

---

19 Mao Tse-tung, "On New Democracy," in *Selected Works*, vol. II (Peking: Foreign Languages Press, 1967), 339–84, at 381. In this short book Mao

Popular governments in Latin America are keenly aware that every revolution must have a clear pedagogical pro-ject and model, because "colonization always starts through culture; decolonization, our re-conquest, also begins with culture."[20] Thus Educational Reform, the most complicated, but also the most important of all reforms, constitutes the essential necessity of Peruvian development and is a central objective of our revolution."[21] The liberatory pedagogical pro-ject breathes life into the historical processes of *newness,* and therefore

> The Mexican Revolution forced us to emerge from ourselves, to confront the truths of history, and to recognize that we must invent new institutions and a new future [...]. The new education was to be founded on our blood, our language and our people.[22]

---

makes countless valuable distinctions for our problematic. He tells us about "old" and "new" culture (354), "dominant" culture (355), "given" culture (354), "imperialist" culture (383), "semifeudal" culture (384), "reactionary cultures" (384), "cultural revolution" (387), "[t]he new-democratic culture is the anti-imperialist and anti-feudal culture of the broad masses" (388), "national" culture (388), "new" national culture (395), new "world" culture (397), "revolutionary" national culture (397), the "revolutionary cultural workers" (397), "the people, it must be stressed, are the inexhaustible source of our revolutionary culture" (398). All these notions, and many others, must be organizing in an explicit, explicated discourse.

20 Héctor Cámpora, *Mensaje del Presidente de la Nación* [*The President's Message to the Nation*] (Buenos Aires, Congreso de la Nacion, 1973), an address delivered to the National Congress, May 25, 1973. He also says that "the stages of the liberation process for the current scheme of culture, scientific, and technological dependence that are used by the educational system will organically determine the steps to reach an effective modernization of the Argentinian school and university, these steps will be in service to the community" (49–50).

21 Reform Commission, "Reforma de la Educación Peruana: Informe General" ["Peruvian Educational Reform: General Report"], 1970, 1. This diagnosis of the educational situation says that everything it notes "becomes direr if one realizes that generally (the pedagogical system) has been oriented towards the maintenance of social order and economic establishment as a consequence of underdevelopment and dependency" (35).

22 Octavio Paz, *The Labyrinth of Solitude and Other Writings,* trans. Lysander Kemp, Yara Milos, and Rachel Phillips Belash (New York: Grove Press,

The people's culture of Latin America, in each of our countries, is a tradition which has managed to assimilate the historical experiences of Indigenous peoples, the Spanish, Creoles, the oppressed, independent subsistence farmers, workers of all kinds, and the marginalized. The people's culture of Latin America therefore has an ancient past, but is also open to an immense future because the community exists separately from the system. The community's poverty guarantees its hope: their position "from below" opens cracks in the system and permits newness to emerge in its exteriority. At the same time, this living tradition is also an historical and communal consciousness which has its own *proper ethos,* forms of life in the home, a relationship to transcendence, a style of dressing and eating. The ethos proper to communal consciousness also includes forms of work, leisure, and valuing friendship through the conviviality of dialogue. It also has its own language, speaking with a distinct personality. The art it creates, festivals it throws, and sports it plays are all marked with its particular character. The erotics of this consciousness is also well-defined, as is its pedagogics and politics. Its aesthetics is innovative, by which we mean its rootedness in a love for the face of the oppressed Other, the way in which it configures this face from the disfiguration of the system's mask. It is a total culture, a total interpretation of existence. A popular song called, "Man's Destiny," recorded by Benedicto Lavallén in Buenos Aires during the reign of General Rodríguez, expresses a moment in the people's everyday world:

Man is born suddenly

1985), 172–73 and 152. In the first half of the twentieth century, José Vasconcelos's thought in *La Raza Cósmica* [*The Cosmic Race*] (Mexico: Espasa-Calpe, 1966), collected under the term "race" that which nowadays (and no longer in a biologist way, but in an ethno-anthropocentric way) we would call community. That is why the Mexican "intelligentsia," for example, "turned toward the people, discovering their true nature and eventually making them the center of its activities. The popular arts emerged again, after centuries of having been ignored" (Paz, *The Labyrinth of Solitude and Other Works*, 153).

and delivered to orphanity
without knowing what will be
in the future and present.

He does not imagine that he is a thing
and his navigating is slow
shipwrecked and lost in effect
and reduced to nothing.
Happiness is declared:
Time only knows.[23]

There is nothing "high-society" about this *machacón* rhythm, whose form uncovers a profound human meaning. The people's culture is therefore not tragic, though it may appear as much at first. Regarding the themes of death and tragedy, the Latin American (particularly in Mexico)

> is familiar with death, jokes about it, caresses it, sleeps with it, celebrates it; it is one of his favorite toys and his most steadfast love [...], he looks at it face to face, with impatience, disdain or irony. "If they are going to kill me tomorrow, let them kill me right away" (from the popular folk song *La Valentina*).[24]

The people's culture, therefore, whose hidden richness has rarely if ever been discovered in Latin America, has a liberatory project: the new pedagogical pro-ject. But an existential pedagogi-

---

23 In my book Enrique Dussel and María Mercedes Esandi, *El Catolicismo Popular en Argentina* [*Popular Catholicism in Argentina*] (Buenos Aires: BONUM, 1970), 151, and extracted from Juan Jesús Benítez, "Cantares de la Tradición Oral Bonaerense" ["Songs from the Bonaerense Oral Tradition"], *Revista del Instituto Nacional de la Tradición* 1, no. 1 (1948): 102–14. See more than one hundred songs and a book about popular Argentine traditions in my book, just cited above, Dussel and Esandi, *El Catolicismo Popular en Argentina*, 167–77, and an initial treatment of the topic between 17–166.

24 Paz, *The Labyrinth of Solitude and Other Works*, 58. On the festive demeanor, written about by so many authors: "We are a ritual people[...]. The art of the fiesta has been debased almost everywhere else, but not in Mexico" (47).

cal pro-ject must be formulated as an ontic project, or model. As the community assimilated the majority of its culture, turning into a popular culture within the system, it has not yet reached this ontic formulation: the theoretical structuration of a project/model starts with a practico-existential pro-ject. "Nor can the people — as long as they are crushed and oppressed, internalizing the image of the oppressor — construct by themselves the theory of their liberating actions. Only in the encounter of the people with the revolutionary leaders — in their communion, in their praxis — can this theory be built."[25]

Thus a new notion emerges: *cultural revolution,* or better yet *liberatory culture,* which itself originates organically in the people's culture. This culture is the fruit of mutual fecundation, both of the intellectual revolutionary (the "teacher" or "pro-phet" properly speaking) and the people on their way towards liberation. Frantz Fanon called the "cultured man" living in colonial and neocolonial states the "colonized intellectual." This status comes with certain pedagogical requirements: "The colonized intellectual who decides to combat these colonialist lies does so on a continental scale. The past is revered."[26] The "colonized intellectual" rebels against his alienated function and compulsions, says the psychiatrist from Martinique, in three phases (with which this very ethics has begun as well):

> First, the colonized intellectual proves he has assimilated the colonizer's culture [...]. In a second stage, the colonized writer has his convictions shaken and decides to cast his mind back. But the colonized writer is not integrated with his people, since he maintains an outsider's relationship to them, he is content to remember [...]. Finally, a third stage, a combat stage where colonized writer, after having tried to lose him-

---

25 Freire, *Pedagogy of the Oppressed,* 183.
26 Frantz Fanon, *The Wretched of the Earth* (New York: Vintage, 1963), 149–50. In this chapter "On National Culture," there are many summarily important inclinations, but Latin American countries are in large part situated in the context of a passage from colonialism to neocolonialism, and not really in the context of this national freedom.

self among the people, with the people, will rouse the people. Instead of letting the people's lethargy prevail, he turns into a galvanizer of the people. Combat literature, revolutionary literature, national literature emerges.[27]

We must therefore distinguish the colonized intellectual who converts to the revolution's "intelligentsia," from the "revolutionary worker of the people's culture," situated at the breast of that same community. Though the latter is not an intellectual, he will constitute the organic moment of the cultural and liberatory revolution. We will elaborate this topic in the next chapter of this book.

In Latin America, diverse political pro-jects formulate pedagogical models adequate to their ends. For this reason, it is not difficult to suppose that nationalist regiments supported by the people (whether those in the center, like Varguism and Peronism; those on the left like Cuban Fidelism; *frentistas* like those standing behind Allende in Chile; and modernized military groups like those in the Peruvian revolution of 68) tend to encourage the people's participation in education — though it becomes difficult to obtain it, since it is implemented in varying ways. This education must be more dialogical, critical of political conditions, with participants from "the base," and ultimately non-authoritarian and creative. As an example, we are told that

> changing the obsolete, onerous, and inefficient school organization on the ground represents one of the most significant structural reforms among those provided by government

---

[27] Ibid., 158–59. "To fight for national culture first of all means fighting for the liberation of the nation, the tangible matrix from which culture can grow. One cannot divorce the combat for culture from the people's struggle for liberation" (168). In this way, the revolutionary intellectual will pose the basic question: "Because it is a systematized negation of the other, a frenzied determination to deny the other any attribute of humanity, colonialism forces the colonized to constantly ask the question: "Who am I in reality?" (182). The intellectual liberator, propagator of liberatory culture, must contribute to this theoretical response.

[…]. There are two key criteria supporting the design of the new organizational structure: educational work considered as a social function of community responsibility; and integration of schools in interconnected networks-nuclear services, with roles in territorial areas."[28]

Thus the notion of "communal educational nucleus" is born with its "communal centers." "Pedagogical space" thus organizes itself with the people's active participation. Additionally, the Chinese experience, though in a different geographical, political, and cultural context, should also be taken into account.

In the same way, in Latin America, a redefinition of the university must emerge from these liberatory pedagogical models. The university must be a place where teaching, science, and technology are presented with a clear critical sense, an ethical-political sense, with the aim of

> preserving and transmitting culture, teaching, educating and training professionals and technicians, investigating and developing projects through the community will be applied to important national objectives to serve the community on the path to liberation.[29]

The child, youth, and the people — as carriers of the people's culture — properly possess the liberatory pedagogical pro-ject. To disrespect their exteriority, to not listen to their novel provocation, is to mire them in domination, tautology, and in the sterility of the "eternal return of the Same."

---

28 "Reforma de la Educación Peruana," 135–36.
29 Cámpora, *Mensaje del Presidente de la Nación,* 57.

53

The Morality of Liberatory Pedagogical Praxis

It is now time to think through the ultimately decisive issue in pedagogics: the educational praxis of domination juxtaposed with the "cultural revolution" of our time that emerges from the periphery. On the one hand, empire — or the "cultured" national elite — is the active subject. On the other hand, the active subject in the "cultural revolution" (which begins through revolution and continues by the construction of a new educational system, which is the fruit of the liberatory pedagogical process in its conjunction) is the child, youth, and the oppressed; the marginalized communities in the neocolonial nations of our global present. That is to say, we must now judge the morality (goodness or evil) of the educational act itself, in light of its respective projects (if it is domination, it is perverse; if it is liberation it is just, good, human, and humanizing). The Other as child, youth, or the people is the absolute criterion of meta-physics and ethics: *affirming the Other and serving him is the good act; negating the Other and dominating him is the evil act.* The liberatory teacher permits the creative display of the Other. The preceptor masked behind "nature," "universal culture," and many other concealing fetishes is a false teacher, a sophist scientist, the sage of the imperial system justifying the heroic conquistador's murders; he is the repressor.

More than any other moment of anthropological metaphysics, pedagogics demands *listening to the voice of the Other*. In pedagogics the Other's voice signifies content revealing itself, and liberatory education can only begin with the revelation of the Other. The student reveals himself to the teacher; the teacher reveals himself to the disciple. If the child's voice, the voice of the youth and the people, is not heard by the father, the teacher, and the State, then liberatory education is impossible. Mutual listening sends, and essentially, the other receives (though clearly with diverse meanings for one party). This sending and receiving is the *conditio sine qua* non of pedagogical love (*agapē*) as extreme gratitude.[1] But if speaking to the other is impossible, if transcending the ontic level of the expressive plane is like jumping on one's own shadow, all pedagogics will remain ontologically situated within the praxis of a pedagogics of domination where teachers and students can only speak with one another tautologically about "the Same," or that which the teacher is. This idea could serve as the inadequate conclusion of a hasty reading of Ludwig Wittgenstein, just as scientism is a false attitude deriving more from unnoticed ethical-politics than from science itself.

Wittgenstein indicates that "the world is all that is the case," and thus "the world is the totality of facts, not of things."[2] A meaning is a fact in the world, from which we deduce that "the sense of the world must lie outside (*ausserhalb*) the world. In the world, everything is as it is (*So-Seins*)."[3] The World, the Totality

---

[1] See the indicated material in section 36 of *Para una Ética de la Liberación Latinoamericana* . Those pages contain a sketch of the pedagogy which we will now think about at another level. [For information on *Para una Ética de la Liberación Latinoamericana,* see the "Translators' Note."]

[2] Ludwig Wittgenstein, *Tractatus Logico-Philosophicus,* trans. D.F. Pears and B.F. McGuinness (New York: Routledge, 2003), 5. It is as we have explained in the first six sections of *Para una Ética de la Liberación Latinoamericana* — with a few variations. The "fact" (*Tatsache*) is not exactly the "thing" for us, but, rather, "the thing" (*Dinge*) would come closer to what we denominate *real-thing*.

[3] Ibid., 86. This is exactly the conclusion we reached in section 20 of *Para una Ética de la Liberación Latinoamericana*.

is *as it is and because it is what it is:* it is absurd to look for a reason or a foundation for the foundation itself. But Wittgenstein (beyond what his neopositivist and scientistic followers say) permits meta-physics (just as Kant does: as a mystical topic, but not a scientific one).[4] "Ethics are transcendental"[5]; which is to say, it occupies a position beyond worldly fact, and, primarily, that of the free will. But "it is impossible to speak about the will insofar as it is the subject of ethical attributes,"[6] because for Wittgenstein "speech" refers only to facts (the meanings referring to worldly objects). This reduction of speech is severe, but at least it does not negate *other types* of speech (though their impossibility may follow). In any case, "if the good or bad exercise of the will does alter the world, it can only alter the limits of the world, not the fact […]."[7] Said differently: the will concerns itself with the ontological and not the ontic, because it can deal with the world as such. However, we must recognize that "there are (*es gibt*), indeed, things that cannot be put into words. They make themselves manifest. They are what is mystical (*das Mystische*)."[8] Regarding the ethical, which depends on free will, or regarding the mystical, nothing may be spoken because it is "lacking meaning." It lacks meanings because it is beyond the horizon of meaning that is the world itself. Thus "what we cannot speak about we must pass over in silence."[9] We must not, for the moment, have any radical opposition to this Wittgensteinian argument (though it appears strange), because it becomes apparent to us that his argument ends when it must begin. By ending his argument there he can make us think there is nothing more to say (and in this case everything spoken is exclusively *ontic*). In

---

4 For Kant, that which is beyond knowledge is the object of rational faith, wisdom, and is the "corpus mysticum of rational entities" (Immanuel Kant, *Critique of Pure Reason,* trans. Paul Guyer and Allen W. Wood [Cambridge: Cambridge University Press, 1999], 679).

5 Wittgenstein, *Tractatus Logico-Philosophicus,* 86.

6 Ibid., 87.

7 Ibid.

8 Ibid., 89.

9 Ibid., 7.

such a case, dominating pedagogics, anti-metaphysical neopositivism, and the "center's" desire for universal scientism, would all be correct. But could it be that that which is *beyond* the world, the mystical or ethical, can be expressed and revealed from its exteriority? Would it not be fair *to remain silent,* and have this silence be the only adequate attitude? The only one from my world about which I am not only unable to speak, but also must not dare to speak? Would it not be just to remain silent about *that which is Other* as a dis-tinct history that only reveals itself from its freedom unconditioned by the horizon of my world? This is exactly what Wittgenstein indicates when he writes that "feeling the world as a limited (*begrenztes*) whole — it is this that is mystical."[10] The ethical, the meta-physical, is only reduced to a thing because the Other is the beyondness of being in the totality of the world (or the com-prehension of being). This Other is a being whose horizon is given, a system *of the past,* a moment overcome in the history of being. Now, at that moment, I can discover from Alterity (Wittgenstein's mystical) the *meaning* of the world from *outside* (from the reality of the Other, of the poor, the child, the youth, the people; or the authentic teacher and liberator).

It is necessary *to remain silent* about that which one cannot speak; about *the revelation* of the Other as other, as mystery, as a dis-tinct world. *"Their"* revelation is "unspeakable (*Unausssprechliches*)"[11] from *"my"* world. Neither is its revelation nor its reality a "fact" in my world. The revelation, in the act of Speech (or better: speaking in the face-to-face) advances itself only in part as a "fact" (thing or meaning: as it is *as such*) but also partly as "exteriority" (thing or reality: it is the *dis-tinctiveness* of the ana-logical). As "exteriority," what is said is the Other as other, as ethical, as meta-physical, as mystical and even sacred. Wittgenstein did not end his logical argument (like Marx, as we see in Chapter X of Volume III, 2 of *Capital,* did not end

---

10 Ibid., 200–201.
11 Ibid., 89.

his atheist argument) and therefore gave way to the negation of the meta-physical.

The *praxis of a pedagogics of domination* is based on the postulate that there is no other possible speech than that which expresses the meaning of the established world: the ontic word of the reigning system, the Rousseauian teacher's word. Dominating-repressive culture, the culture of censorship, practices authoritarian sadism (in the *teacher–student* relation) and masochism (State–*teacher*; teacher–student)[12] as an *ethos*. The good educator, in this case, follows the reigning-dominant culture. His praxis is in concordance with the pro-ject taken by all (the dominators) as natural (though it does not ask itself if it is an imperial pro-ject). His virtues are those applauded by all. The good student must simply focus on repeating the normal conduct of his teacher and remember everything he is taught in classrooms. The ideological tautologies of the *slogan,* of propaganda, of the crushing and dominant myths are the only words. This educative praxis, able to be perfected with audiovisual media, polls and group dynamics (a *dominating* perfection), *technically* imprisons the child, youth, and the people. Education is domestication, learning through repetition, as much in the family (parents–children) as in politics (State–the people). Violence, punishment, and repression teach that rebellion is impossible.

> His being hardboiled and at the same time submissive in the face of real power predisposes him for totalitarian forms of life [...]. The findings (of investigations) have shown that subjects who may be regarded as highly susceptible to fascist propaganda profess an ideology calling for rigid, uncritical identification with the family.[13]

---

12 Apply to the pedagogical what we have analogically — by similitude — said in sections 26–28, of *Para una Ética de la Liberación Latinoamericana.*

13 Max Horkheimer, "Authoritarianism and the Family Today," in *The Family: Its Function and Destiny,* ed. Ruth Nanda Anshen (New York: Harper & Brothers, 1949), 359–74, at 367–68. See 370–71 for a description of the ethos of pedagogical domination: "The authoritarian character's conventionalism and his concern with correctness and the 'things to be done' [...]. He hates

When the father–State is extremely rigid, when the same is true of the teacher, and dominating praxis manifests itself coherently, the child overcomes too much too fast in the oedipal process and identifies himself with the tyrannical father–State. His will remains totally submitted to the paternal and is horrified by autonomy, independence, and liberation. He encounters an ancestral insecurity when confronting the open, similar to agoraphobia. In such cases

> (a) the teacher teaches and the students are taught; (b) the teacher knows everything and the students know nothing; (c) the teacher thinks and the students are thought about; (d) the teacher talks and the students listen — meekly; (e) the teacher disciplines and the students are disciplined; (f) the teacher chooses and enforces his choice, and the students comply; (g) the teacher acts and the students have the illusion of acting through the action of the teacher [...].[14]

We could continue the list of oppositions to infinity. What is certain is that the educator is the *schoolteacher I* constitutive of the pedagogical world, while the student is the *orphanic thing* which receives knowledge. "In the banking concept of education, knowledge is a gift bestowed by those who consider themselves knowledgeable upon those whom they consider to know nothing."[15] The teacher-father-State thereby dominates the student-child-people (recall arrow *b* of Figure 3, p. 97; or arrows *a* and *c* of Figure 4, p. 148).

The dominating teacher has, as the foundation of his *ethos,* a profound distrust of his disciple. This is why he does not invent educational activities rooted in liberty. But injustice manifests

---

whatever is weak [...]. He is violently opposed to self-examination, never questions his own motives [...]. He thinks in hierarchical terms — 'people at the top, at the bottom, and so forth.'... He is a pseudo-conservative; that is, he has surrendered to the maintenance of the status quo [...]. He considers religion important only from a pragmatic viewpoint."

14 Freire, *Pedagogy of the Oppressed,* 73.
15 Ibid., 72.

itself in the magisterial ego through the permanently boastful, lying, hypocritical, and masked attitude.[16] Most important is that, frequently, there is little sense of culpability for acts of concealed and false teaching in the ideological conscience. The formal lie is an affirmation of something false enunciated intentionally to confuse another person. For the ideological conscience or "happy conscience," acceptance of the (dominating) pro-ject's goodness is so naive, obvious, acritical, and ahistorical, that the teacher does, in fact, teach with the best intention, with honest severity, and disciplined stoicism.[17] In reality, all the virtues of the "honest" teacher of the reigning pedagogical system which teach from "nature" (without conscience that nature is the dominating pro-ject of the imperial, managerial, high culture, etc.), are corruptive vices mystified within educational bureaucracy, a castrating bureaucracy, and filicidal. The "honest" teacher of the dominating system is the sado-masochistic mediator of the concealment of exteriority. How can the teacher uncover the real meaning of things to his disciples if he accepts and teaches from the pro-ject that conceals the child, youth, and people as Other, and only accepts them as non-being, as nothing, like a *tabula rasa,* an *orphan,* ignoramus, like material to be formalized: *like an object?*

Very much on the contrary, the *praxis of a pedagogics of liberation* is based on the postulate that I myself never pronounce

---

16 In the Middle Ages, vices opposed to truth were denominated: mendacium, simulatio hypocrisis, boasting and irony. [Translators' note: See St. Thomas Aquinas, *The Summa Theologiae,* trans. Fathers of the English Dominican Province (London: Benzinger Bros., 1947). Dussel provides some citations to the "Questions" in Aquinas's *Summa Theologiae,* furnishing some resources for properly citing them throughout this chapter. We have done our best to cite the questions as they are available in the above reference which is available online at http://www.http://dhspriory.org/. These passages, as translated by the Fathers of the Dominican Province, do correspond to the "Questions" to which Dussel refers. We therefore write "q. 86" to refer to the 86th question, etc., in lieu of a page number.]

17 When he writes that "ratio-mendacii sumitur a formali falsitate: ex hoc scilicet quod aliquis habet voluntatem falsum enuntiandi" (Aquinas, *The Summa Theologiae,* q. 110) Aquinas does not pose the question of ideology as a form of social and political concealment.

the revelatory word of the Other. One can, originarily, hear the meta-physical word of ethics. Liberatory, revolutionary, future-oriented culture is practiced as the free love-of-justice *ethos,* as *service,* as an ana-lectic practice which is a response to the analogical word.[18] Henceforth, our exposition will be divided into three parts and will imply a pedagogics which is *anti-Emile*. In the first place, we will show the falsity of the idea that "it makes no difference whether (the child-the people: the student) has [a] mother and father,"[19] since the child's having a father–mother and a people's culture is the *originary fontanality* of pedagogics. Second, we will also show the falsity of the claim that the teacher "is responsible for their (the students') duties, (to) take charge of their rights…(and students must therefore) not obey anyone but myself (*il ne doit obéir qu'à moi*)," the teacher. Instead it is the teacher, *as critical exteriority,* that "obeys" the student. Third, the *educative process* is not exclusively conducive to the constitutive magisterial I. Rather the educative practice is fulfilled from the student's creativity (the *active subject*) and the incarnated criticality of a pedagogics of fecundity suffusing all the different grades of pedagogical-liberatory institutions. Let us examine each of these three aspects separately.

We must jettison two extremes before we begin. On one side, there is the defective pedagogical situation of the "enlightened intellectual" (the Rousseauian teacher) *that teaches* the masses the path to revolution. Such a teacher assumes a truth which may never be possessed *by* or *in itself*. On the other hand, the utopia of a community that can critically rule itself. This spontaneous illusion of the utopian community is manipulated by either the unscrupulous or the dreamers. Both, in one way or another, want to "use" the community. Every community needs the exteriority of teachers, but of course not every prophet is authentic. There are false prophets, mercenary sophists, "space cadets." Overcoming this aporia — either vanguard intellectual-

---

18 See sections 29–31 in *Para una Ética de la Liberación Latinoamericana*.
19 Jean-Jacques Rousseau, *Emile, or On Education,* trans. Allan Bloom (New York: Basic, 1954), 52–53.

ism or a people's culture that is self-reflexive — will demand that we briefly formulate the ana-lectic pedagogics of liberation.

The first step may be enunciated in the following way: *the pedagogics of oppression as exteriority* (area *D* in Figure 4). This topic was mentioned in chapter three of this book. The child, from the first oedipus, then the second oedipus in youth, the people as subject of the people's culture — all speak *their word*. Their word says, if it is revealed by the Other as other: "I am a *new* history which you do not understand and cannot interpret!" From its limited rationality, the child cannot protest if its words are not heard. On the other hand, its own words are expressed negatively, like a baby's cry. It is easy to silence its voice with a challenge, with a scream, or with corporal punishment. But at the same time the child easily identifies himself with his father, represses the love for his mother, and enters the *machista* world of the reigning culture. The crisis is overcome with the son's repression: the first *filicide*, but for which there is no testament other than the son's primal frustration.

The young man, on the other hand, from his adolescence, shouts as well but with more potency. Furthermore, he can use his long and youthful legs to run, his strong arms to hit, throw rocks, use weapons: this is the young people's rebellion. He also shouts: "I am other! Different than my parents, different than the ancient generations past, than the reigning culture!" This is his word. What is the response? "These boys do not know what they want. What's going on here is that they have not had to suffer yet. They must work in order to understand." In other words: when these young people "function" within the system they will not make so much noise… But we ask: is not "functioning" in the system repressing one's authentic love for one's father and a more just country for the people's culture which today is oppressed and works for the Empire? Isn't this a living death? The young people's rebellion which presented itself in more than fifty countries in 1968–1969, fifty years after the Reform of Córdoba (1918), is not a passing eruption of irrationality. This rebellion is the unavoidable presence of the *new* against the aims of the reigning culture, the presence of those who do not want to live a dying life in the system (death is totalization in "the Same": the eternally repeating ontological infusion of boredom without novelty). This global revolution of the youth, in the United States and Europe,[20] Asia,[21]

---

20 See, among other publications, J. Sauvageot and D. Cohn Bendit, *La révolte étudiante: Les animateurs parlent* (Paris: Seuil, 1968), 2: "They want the revolution, but they do not intend to carry it out in a political party. Capitalist society is the enemy. The bureaucratic apparatuses, the brakes." It is a counter-rebellion, but not only "counter," also in favor of a project they live and comprehend (like all meta-physical pro-jects) but that they cannot express: it is the new, it shall be overcome with a quasi-religious devotion. What is certain is that France trembled as a whole and, in fact, Gaullism itself could not recuperate. The second oedipus of the erotico-familiar situation (like a rebellion against a weak father and in crisis with the impossible identification with the political level (against a bureaucratic system, a new dominating father who, at the same time, is a hypocrite, hidden, split, and in crisis as well). See Klaus Allerbeck, *Soziologie radikaler Studentenbewegungen: Eine vergleichende Untersuchung in der Bundesrepublik Deutschland und den Vereinigten Staaten* (Berlin: Oldenburg, 1973), 246–63. The book by Alejandro Nieto, *La Ideología Revolucionaria de los Estudiantes Europeos* [*The Revolutionary Ideology of European Students*] (Barcelona: Ariel, 1971) is quite complete, and shows the variety of nationalities in the international student movement, the passage from immobilization to renewal, from reformism to revolution, with its supposed ideological foundations (negation of the universalist neutrality of science, teaching, the student-position, and opposition to dominating authority). It is possible to conclude that in the student movement, "triumph is not its function, (its function) is not the substitution of proletarian political parties, but rather to open a breach — as a vanguard — in the system, through which others could enter later in greater force [...]. And since a *new opposition* is expressed, an unedited opening, referring to themselves as new men, there is nothing particular about them employing a new language, a technique and new symbols" (160). This is called the "new left."

21 The concept of cultural revolution is born in China. For Mao Tse-tung, the cultural revolution starts when "the workers, the students, and the new national bourgeoisie" propose a new anti-imperialist and anti-feudal (therefore anti-Confucian) culture, although it is still a bourgeois culture. Mao Tse-tung, "The May 4th Movement," in *Selected Works of Mao Tse-tung*, vol. II (New York: Pergamon, 1977), 237–39. Only in 1966 will Mao send the youth (the "red guards"), supported by the army, to the "cleansing" of the Chinese communist party that would get "out of hand." It was a tactical operation of recuperation. However, the "new Chinese left" went further and critiqued Mao himself. Its members were sent to the camps, from which they did not return nor will they return. Isn't this a case of filicide as well?

Africa,[22] and our own Latin America,[23] shows us from its very

---

Were the youth not used in a tactical moment but also strategically condemned?

22 In black Africa there is a struggle against metropolitan culture, principally French and English, but the youth movement will be naive when facing the dangers of neocolonial national culture. See Jean Pierre Ndiaye, *La jeunesse africaine face à l'impérialisme* (Mexico: Siglo Veintiuno, 1973). This book shows how in Senegal there was also real uprising among the youth in 1968, which repeated in 1969 while it did not repeat in France. Why this difference? "Senghor could not do what the French employers could, which was maintain the advantage of neocolonial exploitation" (88–89). The dependent state's neocolonial power cannot contribute solutions from the "center": they are too expensive and what is more they suppose political and economic liberation. Thus, the student movements have continued in peripheral countries. Which is to say, "the economic situation in poor countries tends to deteriorate, while at the same time the general state of consciousness and education grows" (Renate Zahar, *Colonialismo y Enajenación: Contribución a la Teoría Política de Frantz Fanon* [*Colonialism and Alienation: Contribution to the Political Theory of Frantz Fanon*] [Mexico: Siglo Veintiuno, 1970], 122), which is why we can deduce the growing upsurge of student conflicts in the Third World. Thus the anti-revolutionary war which imperialism wages tends to close the critical faculties of universities in the periphery: the human sciences, sociology (political conflict of dependence) and psychology (discovery of the second oedipus and the socio-cultural applications of Freud).

23 See the study by Armand Mattelart and Michèle Mattelart, *Juventud Chilena: Rebeldía y Conformismo* [*Chilean Youth: Rebelling and Conforming*] (Santiago: Editorial Universitaria, 1970), one developed from a survey—very unique for its genre. Reaching scientific conclusions about young students (poor, middle class, and rich), workers, employees, farmers, and marginalized groups in urban and rural areas, the study opens enormous possibilities for philosophical reflection on the pedagogical. Consider the previous chart on Chile, 1969. The author deduces that the young university student is positioned as "a privileged ideal" (317), such that "they foster a great number of personal and social dreams" (317). This youth which is "self-conscious," yet still free of the "system," is a threat to the patriarchal imperialist culture of the center and the managers of the periphery. Filicide is a boon to so many intelligence services (see the CIA's plan for Latin American universities) as repressive forces (thus the case of Tlatelolco, critically theorized by Octavio Paz, *The Labyrinth of Solitude and Other Writings*, trans. Lysander Kemp, Yara Milos, and Rachel Phillips Belash [New York: Grove Press, 1985], 320: "Tlatelolco is the counterpart, in terms of blood and sacrifice, of the petrification of the Institutional Revolutionary Party"); the PRI, the official party, the Latin American neocolonial State is the son's cas-

beginning a new pedagogical and historical fact in human history: a world culture brewing, global in its structure, which represses the young, those who have therefore not entered the system but must do so soon, and compels them to leave behind games for "serious" work. Their reaction is like someone being hauled off to jail or the electric chair, kicking and screaming in distress. This time of the student is the time when one has not yet accepted the approaching loss of the liberty existing *before* the system, the *pre-historic* goals of the functionary, bureaucrat, of the "honest" businessman, soldier, worker...

The people, in the end, make a more multitudinous clamor. Every political, economic, national, or social revolution is simultaneously a *cultural revolution*. To desire political, economic, or social independence is to desire at the same time the ability to speak one's own language, pray to one's own god, prop up one's own heroes, use one's own symbols... to live at the bosom of the people's culture "of which and in which we were born and have been fed."[24] Folklorism, "rustic" interior design, the return of the

---

trating father, the terrorizing father. Without any warning, the father–State assassinates the youth, the child, as if with vengeance: vengeance against his own castrating father, vengeance for being repressed in a frustrating system, creating the impossibility of letting the child be as Other, free, as a newness, as that which he could not be. Mattelart shows us that employed youth, on the other hand, have a "double tendency" towards "escapism and realism" (pertaining to their position within popular culture); the young workers "some of which might be considered pragmatists" (317). It is therefore necessary to differentiate among diverse kinds of youth. Among farmers, who are more oppressed, there are those with less consciousness of their oppression and those who have more consciousness of their oppression. This will let us understand the importance of the teacher/pro-phet, the critical teacher of liberation. Further, it is normal that when facing the pedagogical system the university student who is more critical is able to express the more challenging truths. His critique is the same critique that the small repressed child launches, the same critique as the employed bureaucrat, and the worker with clearly defined function.

24 "[P]arentes e patria, a quibus et in qua et nati et nutriti sumus" (Aquinas, *The Summa Theologiae*, q. 101): "(the principles of our being and government) are our parents and our country, that have given us birth and nourishment." The people's culture is simultaneously that of parents and country. (Aquinas, *The Summa Theologiae*, q. 101, a. 1).

national mother tongue, the appreciation of local literature (the *boom* of Latin American literature), the dignified self-affirmation of the Mestizo, Indio, the Black peoples of the Caribbean, are frequently secondary signs of the people's exteriority and its expression, which pro-voke a new pedagogics. This expression is a clamorous one. The important thing is to hear it, and become accustomed to hearing it. Essentially, it says "I'm hungry! I have my own history! Let me be dis-tinct! I do not want to be the object of missions, nor civilized education, nor pedagogical methods! Let me be! I have rights!"

The second step may be enunciated thusly: *the liberatory teacher as critical exteriority* (arrow *f* in Figure 4). The man who will be teacher or pro-phet (he who will speak critically "before" the system) starts as merely one more person. At least he does so as an integrated member of popular culture, when he is not starting with oligarchical or even imperial culture. But one day he *hears* the pedagogical voice of the Other (of the child, youth, the people). The ability to listen is already an entire conversion, a "death unto the quotidian."[25] The ability to establish a "face-to-face" with the pedagogical poor is to put *the system* into question, and to question oneself *in* the system. Thus, the schoolteacher's ego of the *anti-Emile* does not demand obedience from the student, but rather demands obedience of himself as teacher to the disciple (*ob-audire:* listen to that which stands before me). This liberatory schoolteacher's ego is the anti-Rousseauian, anti-imperial and anti-bourgeois pact. The teacher is "bound, saving his obedience to his superiors…"[26] The liberatory teacher of the future is led by the hand, blind and weak in the darkness of the *new* world (which is what the Other is *in reality*), by his son, the youth, the people. Only the confidence in their language guides him away from erring, mis-stepping from the path which brings him to the Other (arrow *d* of Figure 4). The disciple in-

---

25 See what we have said about this conversion, only in its ontological sense in *Para una Ética de la Liberación Latinoamericana,* section 33, and in its metaphysical sense in section 37.

26 Aquinas, *The Summa Theologiae,* q. 104.

dicates who he is to him "by signs,"[27] through their relevant and revealing language. What the student is (the child, youth, the people) must be believed, "they believe its absence, yet see its presence"[28]: the Other as other is beyond the presence of things; it is meta-physical, the incomprehensible which does not reveal itself. In my world its face is present, but the mystery of its *new-history-other is absent. Ob-edience* to the Other's voice, and the con-fidence in that which reveals, is the point of departure of the authentic magisterial ego, the *real:* he who will educate. The student's pro-vocative or questioning word *con-verts* (makes convergent) the simple father or citizen into a teacher. This teacher is not born into Rousseau's *pedagogical pact,* with its demands for obedience. This teacher is born when someone, whomever, ob-eys and con-fides in the voice of the person asking for service; the person asking for something needed. The teacher will be *one who serves,* and thus is born as the one who listens to the alterative novelty of the Other.

The voice of the other is ex-igent, peremptorily calling for liberatory work. Before anything else, to be capable of serving and doing this work, it is necessary to coexist together and to be able to communicate. Inability to communicate in a face-to-face, the initial respective relation, must be lived in communication,[29]

---

27 "And thus, through the instrumentality, as it were, of what is told him, the natural reason of the pupil arrives at a knowledge of the things which he did not know" (Tomás de Aquina, "Quaestiones disputatae [Cuestiones disputadas]," De Magistro [Torino: Marietti, 1964]). English: Thomas Aquinas, *Truth, Vol. II,* trans. James V. McGlynn (Indianapolis: Hackett Publishing Co., 1994), 83.

28 "We believe that which is absent, but we see that which is present [...]. So, for us, the arguments for matters of faith are unknown" (ibid., 298). Revisit what we have said about anthropological faith in section 31 of *Para una Ética de la Liberación Latinoamericana.*

29 The face-to-face encounter is an originary situation of non-communication-yet, which should not be confused with the lack of communication between members of the Totality (see Carlos Castilla del Pino, *La Incomunicación* [*Miscommunication*] [Barcelona: Editorial Peninsula, 1970]), where the totalizing modes of incommunication are exposed: everyday incommunication, boredom, routine, fetishism, reification, etc. (69). The kind of "communication" we are talking about here is one which analectically over-

in conviviality.³⁰ Communication is to assume the oppression of the oppressed, to live-with, to suffer-with. The teacher of the future is formed here. Overcoming learned theory, irreal theory, moving towards that theory born at the breast of the people and history itself, real theory, is to arrive in *militancy*,³¹ in the concrete commitment where revelation of the Other (child, youth, the people) brings the future teacher to the praxis of what is believed, but not yet interpreted adequately. He risks himself through the Other as other. Thus, little by little, the other becomes. Thus he goes beyond the horizon of his world and liberates himself from being a functional "part" of the system and emerges in *exteriority* (area *D* of Figure 4). The militant commitment, an adequate meta-physical place, the hermeneutical place *par excellence* (poverty of the historical-real), has permitted the future teacher to grow in self-consciousness, perhaps an intellectual critic, perhaps a revolutionary, perhaps more: a liberator.³² The pro-phet, the teacher properly speaking, is he

---

comes its relevant horizon, to con-verge with the Other in a new moment of "us." Young people have difficulties in owning such a moment of authentic communication with the world of the system.

30 A notion which Illich uses in many of his aforementioned texts. To overcome mere "community" (to become common) by living-together (with-living as a supreme human good): conviviality.

31 The argentine philosopher Osvaldo Ardiles works with this fecund notion when describing the exercise of philosophy and also teaching in general. The "militant" is someone who, immersed in praxis, discovers the need for a real "theory." Jurgen Habermas, citing Lukacs, notes in *Theorie und Praxis* (Frankfurt: Suhrkamp, 1971), 52, that "the organization is the form of mediation between theory and praxis." If this is societally true, then the mediation is produced in the "militant," who is the base of the organization and its creator.

32 The leader of the Chinese revolution proposes to us a new model of the teacher: "People engaged in revolutionary cultural work are the commanders at various levels on this cultural front [...]. A revolutionary cultural worker who is not close to the people is a commander without an army, whose fire-power cannot bring the enemy down [...]. To attain this objective, written Chinese must be reformed, given the requisite conditions, and our spoken language brought closer to that of the people, for the people, it must be stressed, are the inexhaustible source of our revolutionary culture. A national, scientific and mass culture — such is the anti-imperialist and

who will begin his pedagogical task and comes forth only from exteriority, from outside, in precarity, persecution, isolation; the desert.

The praxis of a pedagogics of liberation (*avodah* in Hebrew, service) is precision in speech, unequivocating speech, discernment, it is the "judge of the Totality," the "criterion that de-stroys." The teacher outside the system (area *D*) cuts with a double-edged sword (arrow *f* in Figure 4). The teacher's *ethos* is tremendous from that moment on: if uncritical, he dies as a teacher; and if he lives as a teacher he runs the continuous risk of being the object of persecution, physical violence, factical annihilation, death itself. His death as a teacher is the betrayal to the child's word, the language of youth and the people. His death as testimony of this word, however, is martyrdom, heroic, the humanely supreme death, greater even than the death of the hero fighting for equality in his country. The teacher dies for the weakest, those who can neither defend nor avenge him. The country's hero dies for the present; the teacher dies for the future, for the ad-vent. Therefore, the ethos of school-teaching is the fontanic fecundity of veracity.

Veractiy is not only truth as dis-covery. Veracity is not only speaking truth. It is wanting to speak the truth to those who, in apprehending it, liberate themselves. Thus veracity includes the risk of ideological concealment. It requires a courage which dissolves the fear of speaking an erotic, pedagogic, and political truth which opposes the system. Veracity is a moment of justice,[33] giving the student that to which he corresponds as a

---

anti-feudal culture of the people, the culture of New Democracy, the new culture of the Chinese nation" (Mao Tse-tung, "On New Democracy," in *Selected Works*, vol. II [Peking: Foreign Languages Press, 1967], 339–84, at 382). This is what Paulo Freire, *Pedagogy of the Oppressed*, 68, would tell us: "The only effective instrument is a humanizing pedagogy in which the revolutionary leadership establishes a permanent relationship of dialogue with the oppressed." Without this spontaneous "theory," demagoguery or counter-revolution would devise its pro-ject of historical liberation. This is Gramsci's position, "the organic intellectual."

33 Aquinas demonstrates "truth as virtue." He indicates that "[t]he first of virtues is faith, whose object is truth," but "[t]here are two ways of declining

new and future human. The teacher that teaches the "truth" of the reigning system, the concealed meaning of things from the predominant and perverse pro-ject, neither teaches truth nor is truthful in doing so. In reality he is the sage of the system, charged by the dominators to deceive children, youth, and the community so that they accept the system as natural, eternal, and sacred. On the contrary, he who professes, as his profession, to be a pro-phet or teacher, he who, as his *ethos*, demystifies that which the system pretends to conceal, he who has being-in-the-truth of the Other in order to permit the Other to be itself, other than the system, as his pro-ject — this person will be an incorruptible critic. It is from *sacred devotion* that inspires, for his student,[34] an endearing love greater than any other love. Loss

---

from the truth to that which is less. First, by affirming, as when a man does not show the whole good that is in him, for instance science, holiness and so forth. This is done without prejudice to truth, since the lesser is contained in the greater: and in this way this virtue inclines to what is less. (And this is part of justice because it is directed to another (ad alterum), since the manifestation, which we have stated to be an act of truth, is directed to another (altei manifestat)" (Aquinas, *The Summa Theologiae*, q. 109).

34 Traditional thinking would demand pious child or filial love from the father (ibid.): "[W]herefore just as it belongs to religion to give worship to God, so does it belong to piety, in the second place, to give worship to one's parents and one's country," there is little or no mention of the virtues of the father-teacher viz. the child. Therefore, as sacred Other, we can apply this idea in its strict sense though [with] anthropological relations with respect to the sacred. If there is a cult with one's parents (mine) and country (mine), then to what extent is a relation with the other as Other impossible to create? The teacher must maintain a religion (anthropological religion) for the student (ibid., q. 81), for the "poor." At the same time it must be consecrated in its service ["Devotion is derived from 'devote' (The Latin 'devovere' means 'to vow')[…]. Therefore devotion is a special act of the will," ibid., q. 82]. This sacred devotion that the teacher has for his students moves him to a permanent disposition and service without yielding in truth until death, if necessary. This explains the death of Socrates, and anthropologically the crucifixion of the rabbi (teacher) of Galilee. Essentially the teacher cannot obligate the student through physical coercion, but rather insinuations, conviction; thus one must ask them, beg them (ibid., q. 83), to accept our plea to "be the same." Further, the teacher must "place" signs of his fidelity, must sacrifice himself as a testimony (ibid., q. 85), must know to offer his own life (ibid., q. 86), with a firm and unending will (ibid., q. 88). In its essence, the Rous-

of life through fidelity to the student is more bearable for the authentic teacher than that loss of life-meaning he betrays with students, those who confide in him, when teaching within the system.

However, the teacher does not leave aside precision, demands, and discipline when it comes to the child, youth, and community. On the contrary, with renewed zeal he tries to fight the worst things students have within themselves: the introjection of the system in which negativity lives as oppression, but that in reality is the desire to dominate with those who dominate, to possess the system's values (area C in Figure 4). This discernment prevents the authentic teacher from falling prey to easy demagoguery, staying true to justice and the hard path of liberation. An immense fortitude which must be communicated to the student — is necessary to head up the educative process of liberation. As has been said, to discern the worst (what has been introjected through the system) from the best (exteriority D) is the essential task of the teacher. This is therefore rough work, difficult work, which demands firm judgement and a theory which is both real and clear.

The third step may be enunciated thusly: the educative process, by definition, negates the introjection of the system (destruction) and affirmatively con-structs exteriority through analectic praxis of liberation, in the permanent creative-innovative unity of teacher–student. There is no longer a pure magisterial ego that teaches (educator) and an orphanic entity that is educated (student). He who will be taught first teaches the one who will be his teacher; he is a teacher who teaches the student to critique that which is, that which the teacher himself learned as a disciple. What the teacher teaches is now returned by the student through objection, critique, question, derivation, proposal, innovation, etc. The teacher thus learns continuously from the student; the student continually teaches. The relation is not a

---

seauian or anti-Sarmientian "pact" is a teacher's oath to consecrate (ibid., q. 89) the student's obedience in order to free the student, a freedom mediated through critical service.

dominating dia-lectic but rather a liberatory ana-lectic. As an example, we see several oppositions in both attitudes:

Dominating dia-lectic	versus	Liberatory ana-lectic
Conquistador's attitude	versus	Co-laborator's attitude
Divisive attitude	versus	Convergent attitude
Demobilizing attitude	versus	Mobilizing attitude
Manipulative attitude	versus	Organizing attitude
Attitude of cultural invasion	versus	Creative attitude[35]

Cultural liberation is an action with enormous innovative wealth. The *con-structing subject* of "the new" (in the child his *character* matched to his exteriority; in the young professional his job in a just society; in the community, the realization of its *people's national culture*) is the student himself. What happens is that, to con-struct he must first *dis-arm* what the system imposes (not just what it "puts in place"). This dis-arming moment is what has been called assumptive "de-struction." Which is to say, the mode of expression necessary to negate the negation produced by the pedagogy of domination of the child, young person, and community. In effect, pedagogical dominance (from home, school, university, science and technology, mass media; whether it originates from empire, national oligarchy, etc.), tends to "conquer" converts, members, and puppets whom, by their numbers and passivity, give mass to the establishment's power. To conquer the Other it is necessary to "divide them," separate them, make each person into an island, and prohibit them from forming a group consciousness, whether that be class consciousness or community consciousness. Divisionism makes it impossible to "mobilize," to conjure a certain reflection at the base, a pedagogical praxis; tactical action that opens stra-

---

35 One can see some of these oppositions in Paulo Freire, *Pedagogy of the Oppressed,* Chapters 3–4.

tegic comprehension of the critical problematic. Demobilization manipulates every member of popular culture whether through propaganda, using undeclared purposes, bribery, terror, intimidation, etc. All these are imperial and national-oligarchical "cultural invasions" against the people's culture. These attitudes are dia-lectical dominators because they simply include the Other in the system and introject the Other in the reigning culture (area C in Figure 4). This dominating introjection of "the Same" is the alienation of the other, the child, youth, and community. The father's authoritative force, school bureaucracy, is *total* bureaucracy (as Marcuse would say). Even "life-long education," in this case, is nothing other than the system's pretension to prolong an alienating era of student manipulation, separating the educated person from the people's educational institutions in order to totally absorb him in a schooling that would never end (of course it is possible in peripheral countries for the high cost of this useless bureaucratization would mean).

On the contrary, pedagogical liberation is conscious that the teacher is only a pro-creative subject, a maker of fecundity in the educational process, from his critical exteriority. He will not pretend he has no influence on his students like Socrates or the preceptor of the *Emile*. On the contrary, he will point out the student's creative positionality and will give him a reflective consciousness about what he adds to the educational process, permitting the disciple thus to be critical of the critical teacher. However, the only way to move the student along is to give him something missing from his education: liberatory critique as method. But in order for that critique to not become dominating one must warn the student *how* he can exercise the critique himself. One must "put everything on the table" so the student knows what he is getting into.

The critical teacher *co-laborates* in the process. First, by pointing out what the system has introjected (area C). This introjection is a negation of the student's exteriority, however, it is also a devaluation that must not simply annihilate, but also overtakes: it is an assumptive negation. In this way he will know the system, he will be able to expropriate what is convenient so that he will not have to "reinvent the wheel." Only someone who knows the "system" very well (and thus could become an oppressor within it) can exercise this practico-theoretical discernment, this systematic existential hermeneutic.

The disciple *con-verges* thus with his fellow students, through exteriority, to re-cognize their proper values (those of the new child, the dis-tinct generation as youth, the people's authentic culture). But this convergence must be *mobilizing*. This is to say, it must be able to exercise a certain educative praxis, wherein the risk of their novel exteriorization comes along with consciousness of their destiny. Thus the active *subject* surges forth, a creator, con-structor of the new order. Starting with his r*eal situation* he will be able to apprehend how to build his new world. If always taught a mythical, distant, irreal world he will never be able to grow within reality. The child must discover the hydrology of his community's water system; his father's and grandfather's histories; language in his infantile speech. Young people must discover the reality of the world from their local reality, its economics and politics. The community must gain a critical consciousness of their situation in terms of class, group, and region from within that same quotidian world. Thus Paulo Freire indicates that it is essential for "education as the practice of freedom" to include group reflection with total simplicity "las situaciones existenciales que posibilitan la comprensión del concepto de cultura."[36] Going forward from the discovery of their reality the student must *organize and act,* must structure their praxis, share responsibilities, and, using their theory, make an illuminating moment for their life in common with others.

---

36 Paulo Freire, *La Educación como Práctica de la Libertad* [*Education as the Practice of Freedom*] (Buenos Aires: Siglo Veintiuno, 1970), 151–79. Freire proposes ten situations, that permit the man of the community, by using pictures and photographs of his everyday life — life in the neighborhood, town or place — to discover the real structures in which he lives but had not noticed. From here emerge: "the 17 selected words generated from the lexical universe" of the student (173). These must be the synthesis of their lives, be it cultural, economic, political, familial; in them they must discover their distinct exteriority. Liberation starts from their exteriority.

Negating the introjected, de-stroying it assumptively, is what the subject as con-structor must realize in their creative work. So commences the cultural revolution in a privileged moment of *revolutionary culture*. This is a euphoric moment, a profoundly expressive happiness. In the neocolonial era it is the enthusiasm which the heroes of the nineteenth century showed for building a new emancipated society. It is the happiness from which *"lo facundico"* (as Saul Taborda says of Argentina: the people's culture of the oppressed in our nations, the provinces, counties, regions in the countryside or marginalized areas) erupts as *new aesthetic*. The face of the Indian, Mestizo, worker, woman, child, young person, the face of danger and fear is now seen as hope and beauty: from these arise the future and a new homeland.

To liberate themselves pedagogically, the oppressed (the child of *filicide,* youth and the community of *plebicide*), must discover step by step the new con-structive institutions of the new order. These anti-bureaucratic institutions must be born from below, from the base, from the community. Discovering thus, in an immediate way, mediations eliminated by domination of the "systems" that were built to oppress.[37] Between the looming professor and the intimidated student, between the super-specialized doctor at some high scientific level and a sick person's common cold there are no intermediary pedagogical moments: these have been eliminated. Thus, for example, the *cultural worker* (as an extended version of the educational system beyond the absorptive and bureaucratic "school system") from every block and neighborhood, every rural region, does not need all the schoolteachers' and professors' "knowledge" accredited by a diploma. He can teach not only reading and writing, but can also foster critical consciousness. *The people's medical workers* (one in every hundred people in China)[38] permit a

---

37 See what has been said about the "systems" in section 51 of *Para una Ética de la Liberación Latinoamericana,* like, for example the "school system" or the "health system."

38 See the works of Illich, especially, *Limits to Medicine: Medical Nemesis, the Expropriation of Health* (London: Marion Boyars, 2000), and *Deschooling Society* (London: Marion Boyars, 1996), the section on "General Character-

postponement of consultations with university doctors who attend only extreme cases. In this way the community takes on its own culture, its own health, and transportation, supplying for itself its own services rather than those monstrous bureaucratic "services" (which, at the end of the day, exploit taxes and do not provide utility). The cultural *worker* or people's medic, further, *remain at the breast of the community* for other jobs (shoemaker, bread baker, etc.), which is a much more integrated moment of theory-praxis, and responds better to the needs of the people's culture. The community regains thus not merely the use and passive learning of their culture; the community regains creation and construction of its own culture, but even further: they regain *control* of their own history.

The "systems" of schooling, university, science and technology, and mass media must be redefined at the service of the people's culture. The community must not only participate in these, they must also be in control of them by the mediations of the militant revolutionaries from within their own culture. Peru's organic educational law, for example, tells us that "reformed education has at its essence the achievement of a new man in a new society. This implies the task of creating original conditions for the emergence of new personal and social behaviors — behaviors that are authentically human — and, therefore, are not subject to historical deformations produced by underdeveloped societies and opulent societies, both ruled by money-making, repression and aggression."[39] The new system is called the "nuclear educative model" and includes an adequate distribution of pedagogical services which it might call the "national educational space."[40] This permits a greater participation on the part of the community in taking on its own education by constituting "teaching communities" throughout the country, which among other things lowers costs. Notably, few mention how teachers

---

istics of New Formal Educational Institutions," 108–11, where the reader will find norms for a rethinking of new deschooled mediations.

39 Reform Commission, "Reforma de la Educación Peruana: Informe General" ["Peruvian Educational Reform: General Report"], 1970, 45.

40 Ibid., 134–53.

trained without theory are better-adapted to meet the people's needs. In this sense reform has not yet reached the base. There is, therefore, an interesting "graduate civil service" (of universities, colleges, etc.) in which those who leave devote a certain amount of time in service to the people's education.[41]

The *ethos* of the child, of the youth, and of the community in the process of their cultural liberation can only be discovered when there are authentic teachers who have extreme fidelity in the veneration of their disciples. For them, the student may feel admiration and respect. For them, there is what classicists call *pietas*, which is not "piety" but rather grateful reverence, a love-of-pedagogue, love to he who comes to give the security of an "ego ideal" which lacks the introjected father of the contradictory, dominating, and immoral system. The teacher can be an object of worship when those who hold similar positions (such as the father and the dependent neocolonial State) betray the child, youth, and community.[42] In liberation, on the other hand, the father in the home, the teacher in the pedagogical system and the independent State permit the child to develop their alterative, meta-physical, and dis-tinct possibilities in a creative way.

The praxis of pedagogical liberation, therefore, permits the teacher-disciple relation to grow mutually and become a brotherly relation in a fraternal politics (the object of section IX of *Para una Ética*). The erotic position of husband-wife gives way to the pedagogical position of the parents–child; then this position gives way to a Latin American politics, adult-to-adult relationships in a fraternal community.

The pedagogical is meta-physical fidelity, that of the child, but it is Latin American, about which the poet says well "when I

---

41 Ibid., 179. There are in Latin America diverse experiences that must be taken into account: like the literacy campaign in Cuba, the Costa Rican educational system, and the old work institutes in Argentina between 1948–1955.

42 Aquinas indicates that the pious are concerned with worship of parents and country (Aquinas, *De Veritate*, 294). [Translator: We were unable to find the precise edition cited by Dussel.]

came into this world, / no one was expecting me"[43] or, perhaps, our mother, Amerindian, would wish for us a more promising future than history held for her. In a book by Carlos Fuentes, Cortes's Indian lover would say the following:

They kneel, moaning; crying; embracing; Marina screams.
Marina: Oh, come out now, my son, come out, come out, come out between my legs... come out, son of a bitch... my son, whom I adore, come out... fall on this land that is neither mine nor your father's, but yours... come out, child of two enemy bloodlines... come out, my son, to recover your ruined earth... founded on permanent crime and fugitive dreams,... see if you can take back your land and your dreams, my son, my white and brown son; see if you can wash all the blood from the pyramids and swords and stained crosses standing like the terrible and greedy fingers of your land, come out upon your land... son of the morning.... There are too many white men in command and they all want the same thing: the blood, work, and backsides of dark men... You must fight against everyone, and your fight will be sad because you will struggle against your own blood. [...Therefore] you are my unique heritage, the heritage of Malintzin, the goddess, of Marina, the bitch, of Malinche, the mother.

Coro: Malintzin, Malintzin, Malintzin; Marina, Marina, Marina; Malinche, Malinche, Malinche...
Marina: (*shouting*)... (Pause). You, my son, you will be my triumph; the woman's triumph.

Coro: Malinxochitl, goddess of sunrise... Tonantzin, Guadalupe, mother... [44]

---

43 Nicolás Guillén, "Cuando yo vine / a este mundo" ["When I came / to this world"], in *El Son Entero* [*The Complete Sound*] (Buenos Aires: Losada, 1968), 66.

44 Carlos Fuentes, "Todos los Gatos son Pardos" ["All Cats are Brown"], in *Los Reinos Originarios* [*The Original Kingdoms*] (Paris: French & European Publications, Inc., 1971), 23–195, at 114–16.

Bibliography

Agulla, Juan C. *Educación, Sociedad, y Cambio Social* [*Education, Society, and Social Change*]. Buenos Aires: Kapelusz, 1973.
Alcoff, Linda Martín. "Educating with a (De)Colonial Consciousness." *Lápiz* 1 (2014): 78–92.
Allerbeck, Klaus. *Soziologie radikaler Studentenbewegungen: Eine vergleichende Untersuchung in der Bundesrepublik Deutschland und den Vereinigten Staaten*. Berlin: Oldenburg, 1973.
Aquinas, St. Thomas. *The Summa Theologiae*. Translated by Fathers of the English Dominican Province. London: Benzinger Bros. 1947.
———. *Truth, Vol. II*, translated by James V. McGlynn. Indianapolis: Hackett Publishing Co. 1994.
Aristotle. *Nicomachean Ethics*. Edited by J. Bywater. Oxford: Clarendon Press, 1894.
Augustine. *Against the Academicians and The Teacher*. Translated by Peter King. Indianapolis: Hackett Publishing Co., 1995.
Ballauf, Theodor, and Klaus Schaller. *Pädagogik: Eine Geschichte der Bildung und Erziehung*. 3 Vols. Freiburg and Munich: Karl Alber, 1969.

Baudin, Louis. *La vie quotidienne au temps des derniers incas.* Paris: Hachette, 1955.

Beeby, Clarence Edward. *La Calidad de la Educación en los Países Nacientes* [*The Quality of Education in Emerging Countries*]. Mexico: Reverte Mexicana, 1967.

Benítez, Juan Jesús. "Cantares de la Tradición Oral Bonaerense" ["Songs from the Bonaerense Oral Tradition"]. *Revista del Instituto Nacional de la Tradición* 1, no. 1 (1948): 102–14.

Bes, Gabriel. "Lingüística." *Ciencia Nueva* 26 (1973): 8–14.

Borgmann, Albert. *The Philosophy of Language: Historical Foundations and Contemporary Issues.* The Hague: Nijhoff, 1974.

Buber, Martin. *Reden über Erziehung.* Heidelberg: Schneider, 1964.

Cadogan, León, ed. *La Literatura de Los Guaraníes* [*Guaraní Literature*]. Madrid: Joaquín Mortiz, 1970.

Cámpora, Héctor. *Mensaje del Presidente de la Nación* [*The President's Message to the Nation*]. Buenos Aires, Congreso de la Nacion, 1973.

Carlson, Rick. *The End of Medicine.* New York: John Wiley & Sons, 1975.

Carpentier, Alejo. *Explosion in a Cathedral.* Translated by John Sturrick. London: Minerva, 1991.

———. *The Kingdom of this World.* Translated by Harriet de Onís. New York: Farrar, Straus and Giroux, 2006.

———. *The Lost Steps.* Translated by Harriet de Ónis. Middlesex: Penguin, 1968.

Castilla del Pino, Carlos. *La Incomunicación* [*Miscommunication*]. Barcelona: Editorial Peninsula, 1970.

Chomsky, Noam. *American Power and the New Mandarins.* London: Penguin Books, 2003.

———. *The Responsibility of Intellectuals.* New York: Students for a Democratic Society, 1966.

de Acosta, José. "Historia Natural y Moral de las Indias" ["Natural and Moral History of the Indies"]. In *Obras*, 2–247. Madrid: Biblioteca de Autores Españoles, 1954.

de las Casas, Bartolomé. *Apologética Historia* [*History of the Indies*]. Madrid: Bailly, Bailliere e hijos, 1909.

Delekat, Federico. *Pestalozzi: L'Uomo, il Filosofo, l'Educatore*. Venice: La Nuova Italia, 1928.

Demetrio, Sodi M., ed. *La Literatura de los Mayas* [*Mayan Literature*]. Madrid: Joaquín Mortiz, 1976.

de Sepúlveda, Ginés. *Democrates Alter*. Edited by Alberto Losada. Madrid: CSICT, 1951.

Dewey, John. *Democracy and Education: An Introduction to the Philosophy of Education*. New York: Macmillan, 1925.

———. *The School and Society*. Chicago: Phoenix Books, 1966.

Dorfman, Ariel, and Armand Mattelart. *How to Read Donald Duck: Imperialist Ideology in the Disney Comic*. New York: O/R Books, 2018.

Dussel, Enrique. *A History of the Church in Latin America: Colonialism to Liberation (1492–1979)*. Translated by Alan Neely. Michigan: William B. Eerdmans Publishing Company, 1981.

———. *América Latina, Dependencia y Liberación* [*Latin America, Dependence and Liberation*]. Buenos Aires: Editorial Fernando García Cambeiro, 1973.

———, ed. *Bartolomé de las Casas (1474–1974) e Historia de la Iglesia en América Latina II: Encuentro Latinoamericano de CEHILA en Chiapas* [*Bartolomé de las Casas (1474–1974) and the History of the Church in Latin America II: Latin American Encounter of CEHILA in Chiapas*]. Barcelona: Editorial Nova Terra, 1974.

———. "Cultura Imperial, Cultura Ilustrada y Liberación de la Cultura Popular" ["Imperial Culture, High Culture, and Liberation of Popular Culture"]. *Stromata* 30 (1974): 93–123.

———. "Cultura, Cultura Latinoamericana y Cultura Nacional" ["Culture, Latin American Culture, and National Culture"]. *Cuyo* 4 (1968): 7–40.

———. *Dependencia Cultural y Creación de la Cultura en America Latina* [*Cultural Subordination and the Creation of Latin American Culture*]. Buenos Aires: Bonum, 1974.

———. *Ethics of Liberation: In the Age of Globalization and Exclusion*. Translated by Alejandro A. Vallega, Nelson Maldonado-Torres, Eduardo Mendieta, Yolanda Angulo, and Camilo Pérez Bustillo. Durham: Duke University Press, 2013.

———. "La Evangelización como Proceso de Aculturación" ["Evangelization as a Process of Acculturation"]. In *América Latina y Conciencia Cristiana* [*Latin America and Christian Consciousness*], 74–76. Quito: Departamento de Pastoral CELAM, Colleción IPLA, 1970

———. *La Pedagogica Latinoamericana*. Bogotá: Editorial Nueva America, 1980.

———. "Libros," http://enriquedussel.com/Libros_ED.html.

———. *Para una De-strucción de la Historia de la Ética* [*Towards a De-struction of the History of Ethics*]. Mendoza: Editorial Ser y Tiempo, 1972.

———. *Para uma Ética da Libertação Latino-americana III: Erótica e Pedagógica*. São Paulo: Edições Loyola-UNIMEP, 1982.

———. *Para una Ética de la Liberación Latinoamericana, Tomo I*. Buenos Aires: Siglo Veintiuno, 1973.

———. *Para una Ética de la Liberación Latinoamericana, Tomo II*. Buenos Aires: Siglo Veintiuno, 1973.

——— and María Mercedes Esandi. *El Catolicismo Popular en Argentina* [*Popular Catholicism in Argentina*]. Buenos Aires: BONUM, 1970.

Echavarria, Jose Maria. *Filosofía, Educación y Desarrollo* [*Philosophy, Education, and Development*]. Mexico: Siglo Veintiuno, 1967.

Eliade, Mircea. *Aspects du mythe*. Paris: Gallimard, 1963.

———. *Le mythe de l'éternel retour*. Paris: Gallimard, 1949.

———. *Mythes, rêves et mystères*. Paris: Gallimard, 1957.

Fabian, Johannes. *Time and the Other: How Anthropology Makes Its Object*. New York: Columbia University Press, 2014.

Fals Borda, Orlando. *Ciencia Propia y Colonialismo Intelectual* [*Hard Science and Intellectual Colonialism*]. Mexico: Nuestro Tiempo, 1970.

Fanon, Frantz. *The Wretched of the Earth*. New York: Vintage, 1963.

Fénelon, François de, and Octave Gréard. *De éducation des filles*. Paris: Pierre Emery, 1719.

Fernández de Oviedo, Gonzalo. *Historia General y Natural de las Indias* [*General and Natural History of the Indies*]. Mexico: FCE, 1950.

———. *Sumario de la Natural Historia de las Indias* [*Summary of the Natural History of the Indies*]. Mexico: FCE, 1950.

Fontana, Esteban. "Los Centros de Enseñanza de la Filosofía en la Argentina durante el Periodo Hispánico" ["The Teaching Centers of Philosophy in Argentina during the Spanish Period"]. *Cuyo* 7 (1971): 83–146.

———. "Semblanza Histórica del Colegio Nacional de Mendoza" ["Historical Sketch of the National School of Mendoza"]. *Cuyo* 3 (1967): 43–88.

Freire, Paulo. *Concientización* [*Conscientization*]. Bogotá: Asociación de Publicaciones Educativas, 1973.

———. *La Educación como Práctica de la Libertad* [*Education as the Practice of Freedom*]. Buenos Aires: Siglo Veintiuno, 1970.

———. *The Pedagogy of the Oppressed*. Translated by Donald Macedo. New York: Continuum, 2005.

Freud, Sigmund. *Das Unbehagen in der Kultur*. Vienna: Internationaler Psychoanalytischer Verlag, 1963.

———. *Origins of Psycho-Analysis: Letters to Wilhelm Fliess, Drafts and Notes: 1887–1902*. New York: Basic Books, 1954.

———. *The Future of an Illusion*. New York: Broadview Press, 2012.

Fuentes, Carlos. "Todos los Gatos son Pardos" ["All Cats are Brown"]. In *Los Reinos Originarios* [*The Original Kingdoms*], 23–195. Paris: French & European Publications, Inc., 1971.

Furter, Pierre, and Ernani Fiori. *Educacion Liberadora* [*Liberatory Education*]. Bogotá: Asociación de Publicaciones Educativas, 1973.

García Marquez, Gabriel. *One Hundred Years of Solitude*. Translated by Gregory Rabassa. New York: Harper Perennial Modern Classics, 2006.

Garcilaso de la Vega, Inca. *Comentarios Reales de los Incas* [*Commentaries on the Incas*]. Lima: Colección de Autores Peruanos, 1967.

Garibay, Angel. *La Literatura de los Aztecas* [*The Literature of the Aztecs*]. Mexico: J. Moritz, 1970.

Gellner, Ernest. "Review of Theodor W. Adorno et al., *The Positivist Dispute in German Sociology*." *British Journal for the Philosophy of Science* 34, no. 2 (1983): 173–75. https://www.jstor.org/stable/687448.

Giere, Ronald N. "Naturalized Philosophy of Science." *Routledge Encyclopedia of Philosophy*, https://www.rep.routledge.com/articles/naturalized-philosophy-of-science.

Gramsci, Antonio. "The Formation of Intellectuals." In *Selections from the Prison Notebooks,* edited and translated by Quentin Hoare and Geoffrey Nowell Smith, 3–23. New York: International Publishers, 1971.

Grosfoguel, Ramón. "The Epistemic Decolonial Turn." *Cultural Studies* 21, nos. 2–3 (2007): 211–23. DOI: 10.1080/09502380601162514.

Guha, Ranajit, and Gayatri Chakravorty Spivak, eds. *Selected Subaltern Studies*. Oxford: Oxford University Press, 1988.

Guillén, Nicolás. *El Son Entero* [*The Complete Sound*]. Buenos Aires: Losada, 1968.

Gutierrez, Guillermo. *Ciencia, Cultura y Dependencia* [*Science, Culture, and Dependency*]. Buenos Aires: Guadalupe, 1973.

Habermas, Jurgen. *Theorie und Praxis*. Frankfurt: Suhrkamp, 1971.

Hegel, G.W.F. *Grundlinien der Philosophie des Rechts, Theorie-Werkausgabe 7*. Edited by E. Moldenhauer and K. Michel. Frankfurt: Suhrkamp, 1969.

Heidegger, Martin. *Die Frage nach dem Ding.* Tübingen: Niemeyer, 1962.

———. *Sein und Zeit.* Tübingen: Max Niemeyer, 1977.

Hentig, Hartmut von. *Cuernavaca oder Alernativen zur Schule?* Munich: Klett/Koesel, 1971.

Hermann, Imre. *L'instinct filial.* Paris: Denoël, 1972.

Hernández, José. *Martín Fierro: The Argentine Gaucho Epic.* Translated by Henry Alfred Holmes. New York: Hispanic Institute in the United States, 1948.

Hernández Arregui, Juan José. *La Formación de la Conciencia Nacional* [*The Formation of National Consciousness*]. Buenos Aires: Hachea, 1960

———. *¿Qué es el Ser Nacional?* [*What is National Being?*]. Buenos Aires: Plus Ultra, 1973.

Herrera, Amílcar. *Ciencia y Política en América Latina* [*Science and Politics in Latin America*]. Mexico: Siglo Veintiuno, 1971.

Horkheimer, Max. "Authoritarianism and the Family Today." In *The Family: Its Function and Destiny,* edited by Ruth Nanda Anshen, 359–74. New York: Harper & Brothers, 1949).

———. "Montaigne und die Funktion der Skepsis." *Zeitschrift für Sozialforschung,* nos. 1–2 (1938): 1–54.

Husserl, Edmund. *Die Krisis der europäische Wissenschaften.* The Hague: Nijhoff, 1962.

Illich, Ivan. *Alternativas al Transporte* [*Alternatives to Transportation*]. Cuernavaca: CIDOC, 1974.

———. *Deschooling Society.* London: Marion Boyars, 1996.

———. *Libérer l'avenir.* Paris: Seuil, 1971.

———. *Limits to Medicine: Medical Nemesis, the Expropriation of Health.* London: Marion Boyars, 2000.

———. *Tools for Conviviality.* London: Marion Boyars, 2001.

Jaguaribe, Helio. *Desarrollo Económico y Desarrollo Politico* [*Economic and Political Development*]. Buenos Aires: EUDEBA, 1964.

Kant, Immanuel. *Critique of Pure Reason.* Translated by Paul Guyer and Allen W. Wood. Cambridge: Cambridge University Press, 1999.

Keil, Siegfried. *Aggression und Mitmenschlichkeit.* Stuttgart: Kreuz, 1970.

Kissinger, Henry. *American Foreign Policy.* New York: W.W. Norton, 1977.

le Bras, Gabriel. *Institutions ecclésiastiques de la chrétienté medievale.* Paris: Bloud & Gray, 1959.

Legendre, Pierre. *L'amour du censeur: Essai sur l'ordre dogmatique.* Paris: Seuil, 1974.

Levinas, Emmanuel. *Totalité et infini: Essai sur l'extériorité.* The Hague: Nijhoff, 1968.

Lieber, Hans. *Ideologienlehre und Wissenssoziologie: Die Diskussion um das Ideologieproblem in den zwanziger Jahren.* Darmstadt: Wissenschaftliche Buchgesellschaft, 1974.

Lyotard, Jean-François. *The Postmodern Condition: A Report on Knowledge.* Translated by Geoffrey Bennington and Brian Massumi. Minneapolis: University of Minnesota Press, 1984.

Makarenko, Anton Semionovich. *The Road to Life: An Epic of Education,* 3 vols. Honolulu: University Press of the Pacific, 2001.

Maldonado-Torres, Nelson. "Thinking Through the Decolonial Turn: Post-continental Interventions in Theory, Philosophy and Critique: An Introduction." *Transmodernity* 2, no. 1 (2011): 1–15. https://escholarship.org/uc/item/59w8j02x.

Mao Tse-tung. "On New Democracy." In *Selected Works,* Vol. II, 339–84. Peking: Foreign Languages Press, 1967.

———. "Recruit Large Numbers of Intellectuals." In *Selected Works of Mao Tse-tung,* Vol. II, 301–3. Peking: Foreign Languages Press, 1967.

———. "The May 4th Movement." In *Selected Works of Mao Tse-tung,* Vol. II, 237–39. Peking: Foreign Languages Press, 1967.

Marchetti, Víctor, and John Marks. CIA *and the Cult of Intelligence.* New York: Knopf, 1974.

Marcuse, Herbert. *Eros and Civilization.* Boston: Beacon, 1955.

———. *One-Dimensional Man.* New York: Routledge, 2006.

———. "Remarks on a Redefinition of Culture." In *The Essential Marcuse: Selected Writings of Philosopher and Social*

Critic Herbert Marcuse, edited by Andrew Feenberg and William Leiss, 13–31. Boston: Beacon, 2007.

Mattelart, Armand. *La Comunicación Masiva en el Proceso de Liberación* [*Mass communication in the Process of Liberation*]. Buenos Aires: Siglo Veintiuno, 1973.

——— and Michele Mattelart. *Juventud Chilena: Rebeldía y Conformismo* [*Chilean Youth: Rebellion and Conformity*]. Santiago: Editorial Universitaria, 1970.

Mayer, Reinhold. *Franz Rosenzweig: Eine Philosophie der dialogischen Erfahrung.* Darmstadt: Buchsgesell, 1973.

McLuhan, M.J., and Quentin Fiore. *War and Peace in the Global Village.* Toronto: Penguin, 2003.

Meadows, Donella, Joergen Randers, and William Behrens. *The Limits of Growth.* New York: Universe Books, 1972.

Memmi, Albert. *Retrato del Colonizado* [*Portrait of the Colonized*]. Buenos Aires: Ediciones de la Flor, 1969.

Mendel, Gérard. "De la régression du politique au psychique." *Sociopsychanalyse* 1 (1972): 11–63.

———. *La crise de générations.* Paris: Payot, 1974.

———. *La revolte contre le père.* Paris: Payot, 1974.

———. *Pour décoloniser l'enfant.* Paris: Payot, 1989.

Mills, Charles. "'Ideal Theory' as Ideology." *Hypatia* 20, no. 3 (2005): 165–84. DOI: 10.1111/j.1527-2001.2005.tb00493.x.

Mitscherlich, Alexander. *Auf dem Weg zur vaterlosen Gesellschaft.* Munich: Piper, 1963.

Montaigne, Michel de. "Of the Education of Children." In *The Works of Montaigne,* edited by W. Hazlitt, translated by Charles Cotton, 59–76. London: John Templeman, 1842.

Montessori, María. *Il Metodo della Pedagogia Scientifica, Applicato all'Educazione Infantile.* Rome: Ermanno Loescher, 1913.

———. *The Advanced Montessori Method, Vol. I: Spontaneous Activity in Education.* New York: Frederick A. Stokes Company, 1917.

Morales, Alfredo. *Hombre Nuevo: Nueva Educación: Educación en la Libertad y para la Libertad* [*New Man: New Education:*

Education in Liberty for Liberty]. Columbia: Editorial de la Salle, 1972.

Ndiaye, Jean Pierre. *La jeunesse africaine face à l'impérialisme.* Mexico: Siglo Veintiuno, 1973.

Neruda, Pablo. "The People." Translated by Alastair Reid. In *Poets and Poems,* edited by Harold Bloom, 322. New York: Infobase Publishing).

Nieto, Alejandro. *La Ideología Revolucionaria de los Estudiantes Europeos* [*The Revolutionary Ideology of European Students*]. Barcelona: Ariel, 1971.

Paz, Octavio. *The Labyrinth of Solitude and Other Writings.* Translated by Lysander Kemp, Yara Milos, and Rachel Phillips Belash. New York: Grove Press, 1985.

Pestalozzi, Johann Heinrich. "Semejanza entre el Crecimiento Orgánico y el Desarrollo Humano" ["Similarities between Organic Growth and Human Development"]. In *Grandes Maestros de la Pedagogía Contemporánea* [*Great Masters of Contemporary Pedagogy*], edited by Francisco de Howre, 280–92. Buenos Aires: Marcos Sastre, 1966.

Ponce, Anibal. *Educación y Lucha de Clases* [*Education and Class Struggle*]. Buenos Aires: Matera, 1957.

———. *Humanismo y Revolución* [*Humanism and Revolution*]. Mexico: Siglo Veintiuno, 1973.

Popol-Vuh. Translated by Delia Goetz and Sylvanus Griswold Morley. Los Angeles: Plantin Press, 1954.

Rascovsky, Arnaldo. *El Filicidio* [*Filicide*]. Buenos Aires: Orión, 1973.

Recinos, Adrian, ed. and trans. *Memorial de Sololá. Anales de los Cakchiqueles: Título de los Señores de Tonicapán* [*Memories of Sololá. Annals of the Cakchiqueles: Title of the Lords of Tonicapán*]. México: Funda de Cultura Económica, 1950.

Reform Commission. "Reforma de la Educación Peruana: Informe General" ["Peruvian Educational Reform: General Report"], 1970.

Ribeiro, Darcy. *La Universidad Latinoamericana* [*The Latin American University*]. Santiago: Editorial Universitaria, 1971.

———. *La Universidad Nueva: Un Proyecto* [*The New University: A Project*]. Venezuela: Fundacion Biblioteca Ayacucho, 1973.

Rousseau, Jean-Jacques. *Emile, or On Education*. Translated by Alan Bloom. New York, Basic: 1979.

Rulfo, Juan. *Pedro Páramo*. Translated by Margaret Sayers Peden. Edited by Danny J. Anderson. Austin: University of Texas Press, 2002.

Said, Edward W. *Orientalism*. New York: Vintage, 1979.

Salazar Bondy, Augusto. *Ley General de Educación del Perú*. Lima: Decreto Ley, 1972.

Salomon, Jean J. *Ciencia y Política* [*Science and Politics*]. Mexico: Siglo Veintiuno, 1974.

Sarmiento, Domingo F. *Facundo: Civilization and Barbarism, The First Complete English Translation*. Translated by Kathleen Ross. Berkeley: University of California Press, 2003.

Sauvageot, J., and D. Cohn Bendit. *La révolte étudiante: Les animateurs parlent*. Paris: Seuil, 1968.

Scheler, Max. *Der Formalismus in der Ethik: Neuer Versuch der Grundlegung eines ethischen Personalismus*. Bern: Francke, 1954.

Schumpeter, Joseph A. Capitalism, Socialism, and Democracy. New York: Harper, 1950.

Silva Michelena, Hector, and Heinz Rudolf Sonntag. *Universidad, Dependencia y Revolución* [*University, Dependency, and Revolution*]. Mexico: Siglo Veintiuno, 1971.

Spranger, Eduard. *Types of Men: The Psychology and Ethics of Personality*. Translated by Paul John William Pigors. Halle: Niemeyer, 1928.

Strasser, Stephan. *Phénoménologie et sciences de l'homme*. Louvain: Nauwelaerts, 1967.

Sullivan, Shannon, and Nancy Tuana, eds. *Race and the Epistemologies of Ignorance*. New York: SUNY Press, 2007.

Taborda, Saúl. *Investigaciones Pedagógicas* [*Pedagogical Investigations*]. Córdoba: Ateneo Filosófico, 1951.

Tedesco, Juan C. *Educación y Sociedad en la Argentina (1800–1900)* [*Education and Society in Argentina (1800–1900)*]. Buenos Aires: Solar, 1986.

Trimbos, Carlos. *Hombre y Mujer: La Relación de los Sexos en un Mundo Cambiado* [*Man and Wife: Relations between the Sexes in a Changing World*]. Buenos Aires: Lohlé, 1968.

Varsavsky, Oscar. *Ciencia, Política y Cientificismo* [*Science, Politics, and Scientificism*]. Buenos Aires: Capital Intelectual, 1971.

Vasconcelos, Jose, and Cecilio de Lora. *La Escuela Comunidad Educativa* [*The Educative School Community*]. Bogotá: Asociación de Publicaciones Educativas, 1972.

Vasconi, Tomas. "Contra la Escuela" ["Against the School"]. *La Revista de Ciencias de la Educación* 9 (1973): 3–22.

———. *Educación y Cambio Social* [*Education and Social Change*]. Santiago: CESO, 1967.

Vasconcelos, José. *La Raza Cósmica* [*The Cosmic Race*]. Mexico: Espasa-Calpe, 1966.

Vásquez, Barrera, ed. *Libro de los Libros de Chilam Balan* [*The Book of Books of Chilam Balam*]. Mexico: FCE, Biblioteca Americana, 1948.

Vazquez, Aída. "Problemas de Educación en el Tercer Mundo" ["Educational Problems in the Third World"]. In *Hacia una Pedagogía del Siglo XX* [*Towards a Pedagogy for the Twentieth Century*], edited by Fernand Oury and Aída Vazquez, 225–54. Buenos Aires: Siglo Veintiuno, 1968.

Vives, Juan Luis. *Against the Pseudodialecticians: A Humanist Attack on Medieval Logic*. Translated by Rita Guerlac. Dordrecht: D. Reidel Publishing Company, 1979.

———. *On Education: A Translation of the De Tradendis Disciplinis*. Translated by Foster Watson. Cambridge: University Press, 1913.

Wittgenstein, Ludwig. *Tractatus Logico-Philosophicus*. Translated by D.F. Pears and B.F. McGuinness. New York: Routledge, 2003.

Zahar, Renate. *Colonialismo y Enajenación: Contribución a la Teoría Política de Frantz Fanon* [*Colonialism and Aliena-*

tion: Contribution to the Political Theory of Frantz Fanon]. Mexico: Siglo Veintiuno, 1970.

Zanotti, Luis Jorge. *Etapas Historicas de las Politica Educativa* [*Historical Eras of Educational Politics*]. Buenos Aires: Editorial Universitaria de Buenos Aires, 1972.

Zubillaga, Felix, and Antonio de Egaña. *Historia de la Iglesia en la América Española* [*History of the Church in Spanish America*]. Madrid: BAC, 1965.

www.ingramcontent.com/pod-product-compliance
Lightning Source LLC
Chambersburg PA
CBHW072044160426
43197CB00014B/2618